Snapshots of Lisa

A Candid Look at Down Syndrome
and Snippets of Lisa's Life

Angee Barcus

Snapshots of Lisa

Copyright © 2016 by Angela Barcus All rights reserved.

No part of this book may be reproduced or used in any form without written permission from the author. The only exception is by a reviewer, who may quote short excerpts in a review.

Printed in the United States of America
ISBN-13: 978-0-9973832-0-1

Dedication

To Lisa, who has helped me to be who I am today. She has also helped our family adjust to the different and new, and let us know that there *is* a silver lining or two. She is the bravest person I know, because of all the times she has had to do something that was scary, with the hope that by doing so, it would help her throughout her lifetime.

To my other children, Tammy, Brent and Adam, who immediately accepted Lisa for who she was, their little sister. They embraced her with love and by treating her as they would each other; she learned to survive in the *real world*. To my husband, Monte, who always proof–read anything I asked him to, and gave his honest opinion of the contents.

Acknowledgments

Thank you to those who helped me through this process. First, to the people who agreed to take time to proofread the book and gave me positive feedback to make it better. I loved your comments and truly appreciated all your help. Thanks to all of you who kept asking me over the years, "Have you finished your book yet?" I could not have finished this book without your consistent encouragement.

And, again to my husband, Monte, who put up with my quirky ways over the years as I wrote pages and pages of notes during serious meetings that dealt with Lisa's future.

Table of Contents

vii   Clarification Statement

viii Preface

P. 1 A Big Package for a Small Person

P. 7 Our Helpful, Hospital Visitor

P. 11 Blue Baby

P. 15 The First Day Trip

P. 19 First Milestones

P. 25 Heart Catherization

P. 29 Homebound Program

P. 35 First Birthday

P. 39 Birthdays are a Time for Gratitude

P. 43 Crawling

P. 47 Walking

P. 51 Sitting and Chairs

P. 57 Vision

P. 63 Dr. Non-believer

P. 69 Potty Training

P. 73 The Toddler Program

P. 77 Speech

P. 81 Medicines and Being Sick

P. 87 Ear Infections Plentiful

P. 91 Losing the First Tooth

P. 95 Lisa the 'Unsinkable'

P. 101 Shopping for Clothes

P. 105 Learning to Swim

P. 109 Down Syndrome: Making a Difference in Others

P. 113 First Haircut

P. 115 A Short Haircut

P. 119 Daycare

P. 125 Respite

P. 129 Sister as a Babysitter

P. 133 "She Ain't Heavy, Mom. She's My Sister."

P. 137 Setting Child Free Isn't Easy for Mom

P. 141 The Birthday Bike

P. 147 Christmas Program

P. 151 Sleep Habit Techniques of Lisa

P. 155 A Piercing Experience for Mom and Daughter

P. 159 The Neighborhood School was a Great Choice

P. 163 Going to the Neighborhood School: A Positive Step

P. 167 The Dreaded IEP

P. 171 Having Friends

P. 177 Letting Go Truly Difficult for Mom

P. 181 Girl Scouts

P. 185 Mastering Math

P. 191 The Neighborhood School

P. 195 Halloween is a Treat

P. 199 Food Choices

P. 203 First Communion

P. 205 School Pictures: Preserving Memories

P. 209 Lisa and Roller-skating

P. 213 Winning, Spelling and Soda Caps

P. 217 Size and Ability

P. 221 A Letter From the Heart

P. 225 Epilogue

Clarification

When I first started writing about Lisa, it was shortly after her birth. Some thirty plus years ago, the terminology was different than today's "politically correct" words. There will be times throughout this book when some words are inappropriate by today's standards, but when Lisa was born there were certain words in regards to someone's disability that were acceptable. The vocabulary changes of today are good, because we now speak of the person first and the disability second. I do remember, a few years after Lisa was born, that I received instructions on how to address someone with a disability and the correct way to write about that person. In today's world, I have a mental list of do's and don'ts on this topic, and I try to adhere to it faithfully. But, in the following stories some words are left as I wrote them back then, because changing them now would not stay true to how it was in the beginning of life with Lisa.

Preface

The spirit of this book involves stretching, growing and learning about your child and yourself. It is a lighthearted journey of short stories for anyone who has a child in their life.

When Lisa was born I was already a mother of three children, expecting the routine progression of events. Go to the hospital, give birth, stay a couple of days, then return home to care for a newborn and her siblings. What happened was nothing like that.

Lisa was born with Down syndrome, and had heart problems from the very beginning. While in the delivery room, problems showed up on the baby monitor, which was the beginning of a new journey for our family. Taking her home and caring for her should not have been frightful for a mother of four, but for me it was new to have a child with a congenital disability and I was not sure I was up for the challenge. We made it through the first week, taking her to a pediatric cardiologist when she was a week old, after having to borrow a dependable car to take us to the big city. Neighbors and family members cared for the other children while we made this day trip.

I was already taking notes about her care, writing about my feelings that I wore on my shirt sleeve, all the while looking ahead to see how this could ever possibly turn out well. Writing was my outlet, and I amassed many, many yellow legal pads of narratives. This led me to thinking that others could benefit from what I have learned. I realized I did not have the corner market on having a child with Down Syndrome, but having Lisa did give me some credibility in the area of raising such a child and felt I had something I could give back to others; some insight, some deep-seated knowledge. My intent was to have help for those who might also experience these same situations and feelings.

Over the years, I wrote about all the *significant* milestones that Lisa accomplished. I say significant, because for most children, learning to sit up, walk, ride a bike, go to school and have friends are typical experiences for children. In Lisa's case, we had to help her through these different stages of her growing up years. She is not unique, but her willingness to try harder and do better is exceptional. She has surpassed many of my hopes and dreams for her future, and she has made her own dreams come true. From an early age, she voiced her wants to "graduate, get her own apartment and a job, and to own a cat." She has done all that, and much more.

The book is compiled of many short stories about Lisa and her many adventures while growing up. Some of the articles were first published in a local newspaper and well received by the community. I was encouraged by this and continued writing about Lisa, even after we moved out of state and I lost all contact with those who had encouraged me early on about my writings. Life continued on, and I wrote less and less. The big situations in Lisa's life were still being penned as they happened, but those stories were soon safely stored in boxes, to be resurrected when I had time to finish Lisa's story. That time is now.

I owe it to the parents of today who have a child with Down syndrome and who don't know what the future holds. I owe it to the parents who have children, and who need to know that all children are more alike than they are different. I owe it to those family members and other people, including those who have contact with others who have a disability. There are stories on many bookshelves about others who have had a child with Down syndrome. The difference is that with Lisa's story I mixed in some humor, while I wrote about welcoming her for who she is, and helping her to learn, to grow and to have an upbeat attitude.

A Big Package for a Small Person

After Lisa was born, there was a lot of excitement. We must have had 4-5 doctors that were in and out of the delivery room for both Lisa and myself. We had my obstetrician, who was caring and compassionate, not just in the delivery room, but also for the days that I spent in the hospital after Lisa's birth. My doctor gave us names of some great people to contact, specifically other parents of children with Down syndrome. He was also concerned with our emotional turmoil and seemed to feel our pain and confusion, as if he was somehow responsible for Lisa's disability. I believe he was as surprised as we were when she was born and he had questions because of her obvious disability.

At that time, there were not a lot of tests done during the pregnancy to determine this disorder, unless there was a suspicion on the doctor's part to test for Down syndrome. Today, it is commonplace to have blood work done in the early months of a pregnancy, which can tell the doctor a lot about the unborn child. I also believe that my pregnancy was so typical that the doctor had no indication something might be different. I had had four other pregnancies, one of which was a stillborn son. I did not notice anything out of the ordinary while carrying Lisa, as I had an average weight gain and other body changes that were normal for someone who was pregnant. So, the doctor had no clue nor did we, and for that I am glad. I would not want to know of the disability ahead of time, unless it would help us to be better prepared by having the proper supports ready to be utilized as soon as possible. I would not need to have a choice as to aborting a child with a disability, for that would not be a choice for me. Any child that I could carry to term would be given that chance to be born, and I would care for that child no matter what the disability, as best as I knew how.

Besides my doctor, also in attendance was the pediatrician who was the doctor for our other children. He was there shortly after Lisa's birth, and attended to her needs. She kept turning slight colors of gray, blue or dusky, depending on your color perception, so he kept busy checking her vital signs and current condition. We also had a family doctor who happened to be there; he took care of all our family medical needs, not just concerns pertaining to the children and childhood illnesses. So, he had an interest in this newest member to our family. Our children's pediatrician decided that since Lisa had Down syndrome, a pediatric co-worker of his should be involved since that doctor also saw most of the other children with Down syndrome who lived in our town. Now let's see, that's two pediatricians, one family doctor and one ob/gyn doctor. I seem to think there were more people, but those could have been x-ray and lab technicians who were doing preliminary tests to confirm the diagnosis. There are diagnostic hip x-rays and blood tests for chromosome studies that were done, as well as the obvious visible signs of such things as the simian[1] line or crease in the palm of a hand, Lisa's upward slant of her eyes, ears that set lower on her head, a short neck and her protruding tongue. And as many of the signs that came up with a positive affirmation for Down syndrome, I came up with as many hopeful signs that she might not have it.

I did not accept it willingly, and had to experience the five stages of grief before finally coming to terms with this information.

These include: denial, anger, bargaining, depression and acceptance, which are commonly referred to as the "grief cycle." Even after acceptance, there were times when I really didn't want my child to have Down syndrome, so why did she? I realize now, the Down syndrome makes Lisa who she is, and we love her just the way she is. With the help of all the doctors, (and there were many more to come) and with our friends and family's support, we were able to get through the worst and best of times.

My husband, Monte and I have always been honest about Lisa and her disability, but sometimes not in a straightforward way. When she was born, Monte had the task to call family members. I didn't listen in on any of the conversations, but he said it was a difficult thing to do. I imagine the conversation to be something like this:

Monte: "Hello, Aunt Mary? This is Monte. You know, Angee's husband. As usual, we call you every year or so to tell you the good news. Yes, we had another baby. It's a girl. She was born this morning. And the baby's name is Lisa."

Aunt Mary: "Well, that's just wonderful. That name means 'devoted to God'. She will truly be blessed." (Ok, I don't know how she would know this, but my Aunt was very religious, and I suspect she would know. I looked up the meaning of Lisa's name months after her birth, and even though my Aunt Mary had already told us, the meaning still surprised me but gave me hope that Lisa would be blessed.)

Aunt Mary: "Are mother and baby doing okay?"

Monte: Well, Angee is resting." (Note: he can't tell her I'm crying non-stop or worried sick about Lisa, so this comment is very vague.)

Aunt Mary: "I'll bet that baby's as cute as your other children. Does she look like her favorite Aunt?"

Monte: "Well," (he starts out this way to give him time to think of a safe, yet honest answer. Another quirk of his would be to clear his throat before answering. If he needed extra time to think, it would be "Well, uuummm." See how much time that adds up to.) "Well, she looks like a baby. But there's more. The doctors say she has Down syndrome."

Now, there's silence on the other end, because either Aunt Mary doesn't know what Down syndrome is and has to be told, or she does know and has to pick herself up off the floor before she answers. I'm not sure what explanation would be given at this point, because we only knew that Down syndrome meant retarded, and we had already decided to strike that word from our dictionary. Now we know to say, "Down syndrome just means Lisa will learn at a slower rate than most people." Plain, simple and true. But back then, when the news was still being deciphered and dealt with emotionally, Down syndrome was not something to brag about.

Telling the grandparents was probably the most difficult. Usually they would want to come down to visit right away, help out at the house and fuss over the newborn. I was not ready to look them in the eye and present them with a child who was not perfect. You have to realize that this was over thirty years ago and people with Down syndrome weren't living in the communities like they are now, and many people were concerned about getting too close to someone with Down syndrome, for fear of catching something, I guess.

Whatever he said, the family members he called seemed to understand our needs. We had help with the other children while I was still in the hospital, and we wanted to bring her home to just enjoy her, without other people around. We also knew we would be making a three hour trip to a pediatric cardiologist just two days after our hospital release, so we needed time alone, as a family.

Telling our other children was also a bit unusual. I remember sitting around the dining room table the day we brought Lisa home and talking to them in such a grown-up sort of way. They had been up to see Lisa while we were still in the hospital, so they must have seen or felt some of the tension or apprehension. But, I don't believe my husband, myself or anyone else had actually sat them down to discuss her physical and mental conditions or her disability in depth.

So, here we were, finally at home, with the children sitting in the same wooden chairs they would normally sit in for mealtime, looking at us so wide-eyed and innocently, ready to absorb the information as best they could. Here was a two year old, a three and a half year old, and a seven year old (oh, excuse me, she would remark she was seven and a half) who were expected to hear and decipher what this all meant. We began by saying she had Down syndrome and by then we had the definition for them that we still use today. Down syndrome just means that Lisa will learn at a slower rate. I believe the oldest made the comment that it would just take her longer to do things. Oh, that all of us could see through those eyes and understand with that heart. I believe we were honest with our children, without burdening their minds with our fears and worries.

They were all accepting of their new sister, even though the boys sure wanted a new brother playmate instead of a sister.

She has been a playmate for them just the same, but she was definitely much more than that to all of us. Through Lisa, we have learned about patience, about how precious life is, about strong family ties and about love. Such a big package for such a wee wonder like Lisa.

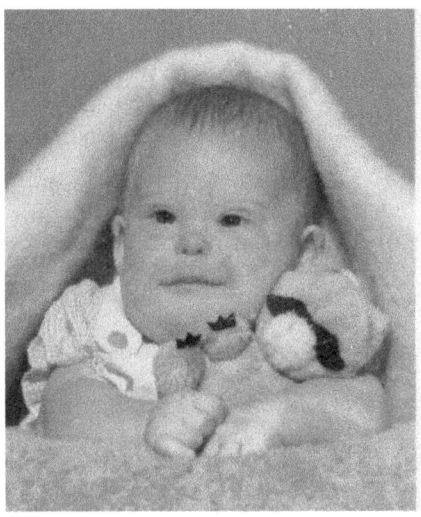

Our Helpful, Hospital Visitor

Sometimes I think it's not what you know, it's whom you know. As far as what I knew about Down syndrome, it was almost zilch. If you've never been exposed to people who have Down syndrome or other disabilities, you have very little need to have any insight to that topic. So, I knew very little. And as far as whom I knew, I was in contact with one adult with Down syndrome, but had not taken the time to get to know that person. Even after Lisa was born and my husband went to the library to check out a few books on Down syndrome, I knew very little because he wouldn't let me read any of those books. They were very outdated and most gave reports of gloom and doom, suggesting institutionalizing the individual as the best alternative. Hopefully now, there is a wealth of books with a positive outlook for the person and their family. As we educate the mass majority of people who don't have any reason to know about Down syndrome, we can inform those people and with any luck make this world a better place for ALL people.

And one way to educate is through sharing. The day of, or the day after Lisa's birth, her physician talked to us about another parent he knew who had a child with Down syndrome. I knew I needed to talk to someone, because my first thought was that I was the only parent who had ever given birth to such a child. You feel so alone, so helpless, so scared to look into the future. So, hearing that another parent lived in the same town was like an answer from God. I agreed to take her name and number, and to let her call me as well to set up a time to visit. Well, I was floored when later that same day she called me at the hospital. I thought we'd be home and settled into a routine before hearing from her.

She came to visit, and brought several photo albums. She also said if her older son was of age to visit the obstetrics floor she would have brought him along. I asked if the older one had, um, you know, Down syndrome. Her answer just blew me away, because she did not have one, but two children with Down syndrome. Now, any of you new parents who have a newborn with Down syndrome, don't worry about any future kids you might have. It is uncommon to have two children with Down syndrome born into the same family. Also, in this day and age there is genetic counseling for parents of babies with congenital issues, as well as testing and monitoring the expectant mothers' progress before a baby's birth. But since I had just had Lisa, and had hardly become familiar with saying Down syndrome, let alone know about the odds, I was not quite sure what to think of this parent who was sitting in my hospital room, telling me she had two children with Down syndrome.

She soon put me at ease, flipping through the photo albums, pointing out their various milestones: sitting, crawling, and walking. The real eye-opener was the pages of photos taken of the older one, and the variety of activities he was doing. I saw pictures of him playing baseball, swimming, and horseback riding. He looked so normal. Had I thought my daughter would look or be so different from other children? I feared she wouldn't fit in or look like anyone else. I feared her Down syndrome would be so obvious that others would shy away from her or ignore her. And now, as I looked through the photo albums, I saw other children with the same disability, going to school, being involved in community activities and doing all those "normal" things. This was the help and information that I needed.

There was one time when I had to laugh, really laugh, at Lisa's facial features. But this was after I had cried about her low set ears, her sloping forehead, upturned eyes and flat nose. It was around the time when the movie Star Wars was first shown on the big screen. The one called Yoda was a very small creature, but a very powerful force. And the first time I saw him on the big screen, I thought of Lisa because their facial features were alike, or at least I thought they looked somewhat related. I am sure I had been thinking of Lisa during the movie, probably feeling guilty for leaving her with a sitter. Or maybe there *was* a strong resemblance. Whatever the case, between the physical features and Yoda's talk of "The force be with you," I felt encouraged by his comments to Luke Skywalker about having to focus, work hard, and maintain a "do not quit" attitude. All of a sudden, I was crying. This was supposed to be an action movie. I doubt they expected anyone to cry. But there I was, tears running down my face, because Yoda reminded me of Lisa, and I felt that we had a lot of work ahead of us, but that in my heart, I knew it would turn out all right.

The parent of the two children with Down syndrome who came to the hospital to visit me gave me some information to help Lisa. I was given a phone number and names of people in the school district who could help. She also encouraged us as a family, to get involved, to push Lisa to the limit, to expect the best from her, to realize that Lisa could do anything, and most of all, to love her. This person also kept in contact with me, and gave me a chance to ask some of those really dumb questions that only I could think of. We became good friends, sitting for each other's kids over time, learning from each other, socializing and sharing. We even had a card club for parents of children with Down syndrome. Talk about an elite group of people.

It was fun and we were able to understand how the other parents felt about certain issues, though we didn't always agree with everything. Each family and each child is an individual and even though the children in our card club all had Down syndrome, they were unique. And that's the beauty of any disability or shortcoming that any one experiences. It makes us who we are.

Blue Baby

Have you heard of Blue Boy, the famous painting? Well, we had Lisa, our blue baby. When she was first born, and still in the delivery room, she seemed to be okay, though I remember she didn't pass the Apgar test. That is a system of scoring a newborn baby's physical condition at one minute and again at five minutes after birth. When it was repeated five minutes later I think her score improved, but still not satisfactorily. They look at heart rate, respiration, muscle tone, response to stimuli, (which means with an action, there is a reaction) and color. A score for each could be zero, one or two, with a maximum total score of ten. I remember Lisa's results were terrible the first minute, and slightly improved on the second time around. I don't believe she cried, so her respiration effort was scored low, and her muscle tone was probably considered limp. Still today, she has weaker muscle tone in some areas, even with all her therapies and weight lifting she has done as she has gotten older. I don't think her heart rate was slow and her skin color, though somewhat in the gray/blue tints, was probably fair because the nurses or doctors weren't alarmed in the delivery room by her color. As far as her reflexes, I'm sure they could have poked her with needles, which they did for blood work later that day, and she would not respond appropriately. She was content to lie quietly on her back, with her legs flopped to each side like frog legs without hip joints, and her arms in a partly raised position above her head, as if in the middle of a bank that was being robbed.

But after the initial findings were tallied, and all her fingers, toes, ears and eyes counted, she was wiped, wrapped and warmed, and placed in a little bassinette that would be wheeled out to the nursery. Before Lisa was whisked away, they wheeled her over to me. The delivery personnel and my doctor were still tending to me as I lay on the cold, hard table, trying to relive the last frantic half hour of Lisa's birth. I gazed at this tiny bundle and held her teeny-tiny little fingers, and wondered what we would do now. She was so helpless and beautiful, and my tears flowed as I remembered the news the doctor had given us about her having Down syndrome.

A little while later, when the nurse was going to give her the first bath, Lisa either thought the water was too cold or decided it was time for some attention, and her skin color began to change to a deeper, dusky or blue color in nature. I was told that the nursery immediately became alive with excitement, nurses scurrying around to help Lisa, making calls to the doctor and monitoring any changes. To hear she was in distress and not be able to go help her just made it even more difficult for me. It was at this time that I started a whole new ritual.

First, I prayed to God that the diagnosis of Down syndrome was inaccurate. It is a human reaction to want your child to be perfect, and I am human. Looking back, I wish I hadn't spent those first few days in such denial, because I could have enjoyed my newborn baby a lot more if I could have immediately accepted her with the Down syndrome, unconditionally. The minute her heart condition became apparent, I moved to acceptance. I also worried about her future, wondering if she would survive at all. So began the bargaining stage. "Please let her live. I can deal with the Down syndrome; just let her heart be okay." I don't know how many times I prayed, thought and wished for her heart to be okay and if that happened, I could deal with the rest of it.

I was concerned about her heart condition, mainly because of the unknown factors. I had some questions like: what was causing her discoloration, how serious was this, and what do I need to know. I wasn't real sure about how to do CPR,[2] technically known as cardiopulmonary resuscitation, and I really wanted to review that. I wondered if she needed any medicine or special equipment to go home with her. But the doctor reassured me that we did not need to be concerned, because since she hadn't quit breathing while in the hospital, it was unlikely to happen at home. Changing colors was a symptom of something not being right, but in itself not a health concern. We took her home with great anticipation, hesitation and with this advice from the doctor, "to love her and get to know her."

At one week old Lisa was in the big city, at a large hospital, being seen by a pediatric cardiologist. She slept a lot that day, even through all the exams she had. We were at a teaching hospital, so every intern, resident or new student who may have been even remotely connected to cardiology and pediatrics, or maybe just any doctor who *had* to take a listen to Lisa's heart beat, did. I guess by this time her heart condition was called a murmur, which mimics the sound of a soft, blowing or rasping noise heard with a stethoscope. They were not sure how severe this was or even the cause. There was the mention of one hole in the top of her heart, and that was enough to scare me, but the specialist just said we would monitor her progress. That scared me even more. She was seen in that hospital every few months in addition to her regular new baby visits back at home. Each time, doctors said something a little different. One time, she had a hole in the bottom part of her heart, and then it was two holes, then one large one and so on. Still, it was "We will monitor her." Finally, some eight months after her birth, she was ready for a heart catherization[3] and an echocardiogram[4] to have a definite diagnosis. The catherization procedure consisted of having the doctor thread a tube through a leg vein and up into the heart to detect her abnormality. The echocardiogram is noninvasive, because it uses ultrasound to see the internal cardiac structures. With this test, they can see the valves and different chambers of the heart.

We were shown the results on a television screen, but all I could see was a bunch of dark shapes and lines, some moving like the flippers on a pinball machine and other shapes that looked like a partially deflated balloon that would slightly inflate, followed by return to its original size. This was all done very quickly, over and over again. We bobbed our heads in acknowledgment of the doctor's explanation and took her home after that day's ordeal. That was the best feeling I could ever experience.

The First Day Trip

Within hours of Lisa's birth, it was very evident she had a heart condition. Either that or she knew my favorite color was blue, and she decided to change her skin color from a natural skin tone to blue and dusky gray. At first, it was very scary to see this happen but over time, it either got better or we got use to it.

There were all kinds of guesses as to the exact problem, and until her heart catherization was performed when she was eight months old, we had to listen to a lot of doctors and a lot of guesses. They could determine a lot from just listening to her heart, with all its whooshes and swishes of blood flow, but it seemed to change just enough to keep those doctors on their toes.

When Lisa was one week old, we planned our first of many day trips to the big city some three hours away. The trip itself was uneventful, because Lisa slept all the way and the borrowed car ran smoothly and quietly. I wanted to have Lisa dry and well fed before the visit, but I couldn't wake her enough for her to drink a bottle. I made a mental note to ask about the amount of time she spent sleeping. I wondered if it was related to her heart or her Down syndrome, but either way I thought she should be awake more. Boy, I just didn't know when I had it so good. A sleeping baby is nothing to question. The diaper got changed as we sat in the parking lot and stared up at the huge medical facility. It was a teaching hospital, and I should have had a clue about what that visit would entail. I only thought about the worst case scenario and the fact that Lisa was probably so bad that we'd have to okay surgery right then and there. Our wait in the office lobby was not too long. I noticed a few other small babies and children, which made me wonder what their medical problem might be. When our turn came, we were escorted down a long narrow hall with lots of doorways every few feet. It felt like being in one of those dreams where you keep walking and the hallway has many doors on both sides of the hallway, and it never ends no matter how far down you walk. We finally reached our little room near the end of the hall. The room seemed to be no bigger than a bathroom. I don't remember any windows, and it had a really closed-in feeling. And by the time we had several other people in there, it felt more like a coat closet with no room to move around.

At a week old Lisa was not interested in anything except sleep, so she tolerated all the poking and prodding. We were set up to see one specific pediatric cardiologist, but every doctor who had any interest in this field seemed to come in to listen to her heart. It must have sounded unusually abnormal because each time one doctor or resident listened to her, their facial expression changed to one of disbelief or curiosity and invariably they would make some comment about the various heart sounds and actions of the heart. Such words included the rate, cardiac output, murmurs heard, systolic, diastolic, atria, ventricles, bruits and so on. Their exam was thorough in the beginning, and then it just seemed to be pointless to me. One doctor or resident would just look up from the exam and pronounce, "You know, so and so should hear this." And just that quick, off they'd go, to get the next person who needed to listen. They all did several standard procedures: such as auscultation that shows the intensity, quality and rhythm of heart sounds, and maybe it's even to listen to murmurs. All seemed intent on this, listening very carefully, hearing the "lub-dub" or swish noises. It all meant something to them. They kept saying how unusual or loud it sounded, and there were suspicions of two holes, one in the upper chambers(atria) and one in the lower chambers (ventricle). That was an ongoing discussion.

This was our first trip here and was a very long day. We were told to monitor her progress through our hometown pediatrician, and to return in two to three months. I don't even believe Lisa had any tests run; no labs or anything else, just the exam by everyone who was anyone in cardiology. They just told us to come back. Wow, was I surprised. I had expected the worst; either she was dying and we couldn't do anything, or she needed immediate surgery and we'd have to make some major decisions. My husband and I had already discussed what we would do if she needed surgery. There was no question about it, we would agree to do whatever it took to save her. Now some people would argue that she had Down syndrome, and therefore we could choose not to do anything, which could mean to "let her die." Well, this was not the way we felt. In fact, we had checked with other family members about borrowing money, and we even went to the bank to discuss possible loans for surgery if necessary. Now, they were telling us to take her home and we'd have regular check-ups. With such good news, we wanted to have a "mini" celebration, so we went to eat at Red Lobster.

You have to remember, we had just brought home our fourth child, I was a stay-at-home mom, and there was very little extra money at that time. Yet we splurged by going to this restaurant that we normally couldn't afford. Lisa had a report from the doctors much better than we expected, and it was news worth celebrating.

Lisa slept through the meal, but my husband and I enjoyed it and began to look at the future with a much better attitude. The only problem was what to do to celebrate on each subsequent visit. And there were lots of visits. We had now set precedence. How could we not go there to eat after our next visit to the big city? It became evident that we couldn't continue the tradition to eat at Red Lobster after every appointment Lisa had at this hospital, due to expenses, some which included many other doctors' visits and prescription medicines.

That first trip will always be memorial, because we had seen only a bleak future for Lisa if her heart condition was serious, and instead we were able to celebrate her one week of life, with hope for a great future. And we ate at the Red Lobster.

First Milestones

A baby's milestones, or their *firsts* of a successful try at something new, have a timeline which most babies follow fairly close. You know, skills like holding their head up, rolling over, sitting up, crawling, walking, and usually in that order. Lisa was no exception to this timeline, at least in the beginning. She held her head up fairly well at an early age, even though it looked like a real struggle on her part. First, she could barely lift her head when lying on the floor on her stomach. It was also such an effort to turn her head from one side to the other. I always worried about her tiny nose, thinking she would rub it to a nub when turning her head side to side while on the floor. It was probably a good thing her nose was so tiny, or it could have been a hazard in her head turning abilities. I'm sure she accomplished this skill within days because I don't remember physically having to turn her head to give her new scenery.

Because of the state we lived in, when Lisa was three months old she began "school," having a homebound[5] teacher come to our home three days a week. This certified teacher would analyze Lisa's abilities and needs, then instruct us on certain techniques that would help Lisa in her advancements. After learning to hold her head up by herself, the next skill was for her to lie on her stomach and lift her head for longer periods of time, to just look around and strengthen those neck muscles. This was more of a challenge, so we all helped to encourage her progress.

We first had to find something that would get her attention, and encourage her to look up. One of her favorite toys that did just that was a bright orange, prickly-looking, plastic, squeaky porcupine.

Lisa loved to hear it squeak, and she giggled when we rubbed the prickly extensions on her arms and hands. That became her focal point. At first, we placed it to one side to catch her attention. Gradually, we moved it more out in front of her, where she would have to pick up her head to see it. Lisa would lift her head when still in the "turned to the side" position and at that point, she would adjust her head to be more in alignment with her spine and body. To keep her head up off the floor took more encouragement. We would set the porcupine on a small block and later a more elevated box, to continue her head lifting. She was not like any of my other babies. It was to Lisa's benefit to be taught and prodded to learn the things that most babies automatically did on their own. Granted, she would eventually do these on her own, but by helping her to stay on track for these gross motor milestones, she would achieve some of the objectives a little earlier.

The prone incline board that all of the siblings helped to build was great for this activity. She seemed comfortable on it and we just continued to place the object higher than she was, to encourage a heads up position. Later on, we would have her situated on the prone board and place something just out of her reach, with her arms stretched out and her head lifted up. Good muscle building!

Lisa also had to learn to hold her torso up off the ground, like in an "army crawl" position. The forearms would be on the floor, bent at the elbows. There would be an open space under her upper chest if she held herself up properly. But, Lisa tended to use one arm in this position, with the other flat on the floor, and she would pull herself forward in a lopsided sort of way.

Now that she could hold her head up, she was ready to start rolling over. She had been trying to do so out of instinct, I think, but she didn't have any real success until she was almost three months old. She would lift her head up really high and slowly start to lean over, using the weight of her head. She also used the opposite arm to push in the direction she was leaning. She could spend hours in this position without ever rolling completely over to her back.

The very first time she rolled over was extra special, because Lisa's grandfather, (my dad) was the first to see her accomplish this feat. We were visiting one weekend and Lisa had just spent several hours on a long car trip, in her car seat. I'm sure she was glad to be able to stretch out on the floor. I had just shown my Dad how we were working on helping Lisa with rolling, and I went through the motions, both to the left and right, several times for him and Lisa. One of her problem areas was her legs. She'd get part way over, but her feet would tangle or get crossed, which in turn would somehow suspend her more on her side than necessarily, and it hindered her from completely getting rolled over onto her back. She would have to remain that way until someone would uncross her legs and with that little bit of help, over she'd go. The home bound teacher wouldn't give her credit for partial completion, so we had to let her try to do it all on her own, no matter how long it took her to get untangled.

On the day she finally succeeded, from start to finish, to roll from her stomach to her back, my Dad saw it first. I didn't believe she completed the task, even when my Dad said he was witness to the triumph. I had walked out of the room and within minutes my Dad was telling me to come and look at Lisa. There she was on her back, and looked as pleased as punch for her accomplishment. I asked my Dad if he helped but he said no. I rolled her back onto her stomach, and waited and waited. I was just about ready to leave the room when it happened again. It looked like slow motion; she lifted her head up high, and slowly leaned to the right. I remember this because she rolled to the right long before she rolled to the left. Ever so slowly she began to fall over, and with a little back and forth rocking motion, using her left arm and leg, she completed the task, ending on her back without the tangled feet. There was a lot of hand clapping and positive, verbal reinforcement from both my Dad and I. Then I rolled her right back onto her stomach. Now I guess I was pushing it, expecting her to do this over and over for me. But, it was so great to watch.

    Her rolling over to the left took longer for her to master, and rolling from her back onto her stomach even more delayed. That was real tricky because she couldn't use the weight of her head for leverage. In fact, we use to position her arms to allow for easier maneuverability. You realize how difficult it is to roll over your arm when you try it yourself. It took some very calculated positions with Lisa's arms and legs, and lots of practice, before she became a pro at rolling. Once she mastered this skill there was no stopping her, unless she got caught under an end table or another piece of furniture that seemed to get in the way. Every baby milestone for Lisa was a personal accomplishment for all of us who helped her, prodding and pushing her, prompting and encouraging her every step of the way. She was pushed to her limit and surpassed all our expectations. She accepted these challenges, and always tried to do her very best. These early accomplishments set her on a course for a bright and capable future. We didn't doubt it could be; we expected Lisa to do her best each and every time she worked on something new, and she has always stepped up to the challenge.

BARCUS

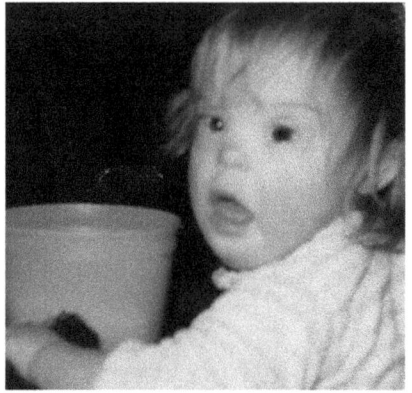

Heart Catherization

The Taber's Encyclopedia Medical Dictionary, 16 Edition, says this about cardiac catherization: "Passage of a tiny plastic tube into the heart through a blood vessel. Samples of blood are withdrawn for testing; blood pressure and cardiac output are measured. Used in diagnosis of heart disorders and anomalies." Under the nursing implications it says to prepare the patient physically and emotionally for the procedure. What they didn't say was the mom and dad should also be prepared. I'm sure the doctor explained everything to us ahead of time, and the nurses were also helpful before and after the procedure. I just wasn't ready emotionally.

We had known for some time that Lisa needed a heart catherization because since her birth, the doctors were not quite sure how serious her condition was or what exactly was wrong with Lisa's heart. Each visit to the doctor had us wondering, so when she was eight months old it was decided to go ahead with this procedure. She had an echocardiogram when she was a baby, but no invasive procedures. The echo is a noninvasive method of using ultrasound to visualize the internal cardiac structures. They measure dimensions and look at the valves. There is a hand-held, wand-type piece of equipment that is lubricated and firmly pressed against the chest in various positions to get the different views of the heart. I remember being told that she would have to be very still during this process, which could be a problem for a baby. But Lisa, taking everything in stride, actually slept through her first echocardiogram. The second echo later on was a little more difficult because she was a little older, didn't sleep as often, and she was less tolerant of the poking and prodding. I tried to give her a bottle ahead of time, hoping she would be content and with a bit of luck, tired with a full tummy. It didn't help. All I managed to do was give her ammunition to "urp" up at will to anyone handling her, even on me. I was told she really couldn't be sucking on the bottle during the procedure because of possible interference. She did get through it, but not as easily as when she was a newborn.

Now, for the heart catherization she had to lie still because of the type of procedure it entailed. As it turned out, they anesthetized her and made it so much better for her. But not for me. No matter how much you prepare for something like that, you just can't know everything that will go on. It was real tough letting them give her a shot to promote drowsiness. She and I both cried. Soon it was time for her to go to the procedure room. I was holding her in my arms, so I walked with the nurse to the elevator and rode down to the operating room floor before finally handing her over. It was like letting go; the first of many times to come. The waiting was the hardest part. We had to sign papers to give permission for this procedure, and the usually disclaimers were there if something goes wrong, etc. etc. Now, sitting in the waiting room had me rethinking what actually could go wrong, and that didn't help my state of worry. I should have read all the *etceteras* a little more closely.

Several of my older sisters had driven two to three hours to be there, along with my mom and dad. We had to drive in from our hometown the night before for some preliminary tests, and stayed in a facility for family members. I had left Lisa in the care of the nurses in a double occupancy room, and I tried to sleep in another wing of the hospital building as the nurses suggested. Now, sitting in the waiting room, I wished I had stayed by her side the night before. I thought I must have looked like an uncaring mom who didn't stand by the crib all night like some of the other moms. I should have stayed near her all night, stayed awake like a sentry, watching her and caring for her. The nurses had reassured me that she would be fine and that I should go have a quiet and peaceful rest before the next day's procedure. I was now sitting in the waiting room, feeling guilty for not being with her the night before. Guilt and worry kept me busy during the entire procedure.

I can say I was certainly glad when a nurse came to tell us the procedure was over and Lisa was doing just fine. The results showed Lisa had a hole in the bottom part of her heart, between the two ventricles. And as usual, the directions were to monitor her progress. There was talk that she may never need surgery and that the hole may close on its own. The main precaution back then was for prophylaxis[6] medicine before any dental work, to guard against infection.

It was like a weight being lifted from our shoulders, just to be told that her heart condition was stable, and treatable if it ever became an issue. When they brought her back to the room after the procedure, she seemed to be okay. No grogginess, no crying, no ill effects. There was a small Band-Aid in the upper right groin area, in the depression between the thigh and the trunk of the body. It had to be checked to make sure she didn't start to bleed. So here was my next targeted area of worry. I kept her still by holding her a lot, and it made me feel like I was doing my part. After having to worry about possible surgery, it was nice to just have to monitor a Band-Aid.

Her heart still has a hole in it, but there are indications it has closed a little with each passing year. It may never close completely but that is okay because she can live with a hole if it's not a bother physically. I have found other things to worry about, because that's my nature, I guess. And besides, I've discovered that most of the things I worry about never develop, so my worrying must help.

Homebound Program:
Helping Parents Develop Their Child's Potential

The world of special education is an array of services geared to helping children achieve their highest potential. Being exposed to all the choices available is mind-boggling. Just figuring out the acronyms takes a carefully compiled dictionary. Even from state to state, there are some differences in what is offered and when.

We were fortunate enough to be living in Nebraska when Lisa was born, at a time when services began at birth. Not all states offered this for that young age group in the special services through the school system. It was also advantageous that Lisa was born a few years after PL 94-142, a major law to "insure that all handicapped children have a free and appropriate public education which includes special education and related services to meet their unique needs." This act also desired to "..insure that the rights of handicapped children and their parents are protected." In 1990, PL94-142 was amended, and was then know as 1990 Individuals with Disabilities Act (IDEA). It guaranteed "that all children with disabilities have available to them...a free appropriate public education which emphasizes special education and related services designed to meet their needs." The law goes on to list how the goals would be met.

I am grateful that we had older children who were already in school. This helped us later on, by knowing people in the field of education who became a real asset when it came to dealing with school issues relating to Lisa. But, when she was a newborn, we knew of no one in the special services educational field, and had to rely on advice and guidance of our new friends, which were parents of children with Down syndrome.

To get started with this program, I first had to call the number I was given, which was for the building that later became a familiar place for our family, when Lisa, at the ripe old age of three, attended the preschool there. There were others who pointed to the building and would remark that it was the "old building where the disabled students go." That was not entirely the situation with the building, because it mostly housed administration for the special educational services. Yet people continued to label that building as different. It was my first experience with feeling segregated and different from other parents.

I set up an initial visit for someone to come to the house who would help me fill out some paperwork, and to visit about Lisa, the school's programs and opportunities available to her. After that first visit, Lisa was considered "enrolled" in school. It was pretty wild, telling people that my three month old was in school. She didn't leave the house for this either; the teachers came to her. There were several different teachers over the course of three years, in the areas of physical and occupational therapy, speech therapy and a homebound teacher. At three months of age, Lisa was in "school," and I was pretty proud of that. Later on, I found out there was one other baby even younger than Lisa, who was enrolled and being helped at one week of his early life.

At first I was surprised to find out there was schooling available for a newborn. What would they do with a baby? What could newborns do? I tried to envision babies being taught, like in a classroom setting, but only came up with ridiculous cartoon images.

Even with all my questions and skepticism, Lisa's experiences with early education were very helpful, supportive and encouraging. It gave her the best start to become who she is today.

What kinds of things can a 3-month old child accomplish? As a mother of three children before Lisa's birth, I thought most babies just ate and slept a lot. Would you believe they also have many skills at this young age and have acquired them without any help? We were told Lisa would need help to achieve some of these same skills, so by the age of 3 months she was in school, aptly named the Homebound Program.

Before starting with the program, a certified, homebound schoolteacher visited us at our home, evaluated Lisa and told us about Lisa's present skills. She already had many skills I had taken for granted. She could hold her head up for awhile, babbled nonsense sounds and had some control of her motor abilities. From the teacher evaluation and other observations, goals were set for Lisa and we were encouraged to help her. We worked on physical and mental capabilities such as motor control, social skills and communication.

The family made a commitment to help in every way, and we worked on those various goals established for Lisa. We were shown how to work with her and tried to do so daily. These goals were changed as often as she mastered them; each goal was more detailed and difficult. Knowing what she could do and what to work on in the future helped us with the schedule and to keep abreast of goals that were accomplished. With hope, prayers and a lot of work most realistic goals would be met.

The Homebound Program made it possible for many

children to have the opportunity to learn more consistently and possibly at a faster rate. Lisa would probably have mastered some of these skills on her own, but the focused help contributed to her accomplishing the goals at a more appropriate age level. With these special-age related programs, children with disabilities were no longer being left in cribs or playpens to just exist. They were helped to develop whatever abilities they had to their fullest potential. With the help of such programs, parents could become more involved with their child's growth and development.

With many of Lisa's objectives, we would brainstorm to come up with different techniques to help her. Her weekly activities were easily incorporated into our daily routine. We would run through any new activities with our other children, and they could also work with her at will. The boys even helped make a piece of equipment for Lisa to use. Her assignment was to hold her head up by herself. I remember she did that in the hospital when she was lying on her stomach, so I thought she really didn't need to work on that. But I was told for her to learn to sit up on her own, this was the first step of many. Lisa's Dad and her two brothers built an incline support similar to a car ramp, with the height on one end at about 3-4 inches, while the end where Lisa's feet would be was just an inch off the floor. Lisa's sister helped to cover it with material to give it a soft, "comfy" pad to lie on and have it look attractive as well. The finished project was a nice wooden prone board used to keep her on her stomach in an incline position.

Lisa would lie on her stomach on the slanted board, and it helped to strengthen her neck and shoulder muscles, which helped her to learn to hold her head up. It must have helped because she was right on track with most of the typical baby milestones like rolling over and sitting. This incline came in handy later on for other activities, and gave her a nice position change. This was also something the entire family was involved with, and brought us closer together, knowing we were helping Lisa to be the best she could be. We have always encouraged Lisa from the very beginning, to try harder, to do her best. We never said she couldn't do something because she had Down syndrome. Instead, we might have seen the challenge and said why she should try it. We never knew what she could accomplish and we figured you get what you expect, so always expect more. Time and time again we were pleasantly surprised.

I am afraid that without this super program and its support to the family, many children would have been neglected, having little or no outside stimulation. Parents would be unaware of how to develop their child's skills and they would never know their child's true potential.

The Homebound Program was just the first step to many years of special education services available for Lisa. She and many others have probably had many successes in their lifetime because of programs like this. This program was just one of many offered at the school system. Lisa was involved in during her early years. It was a great start for Lisa.

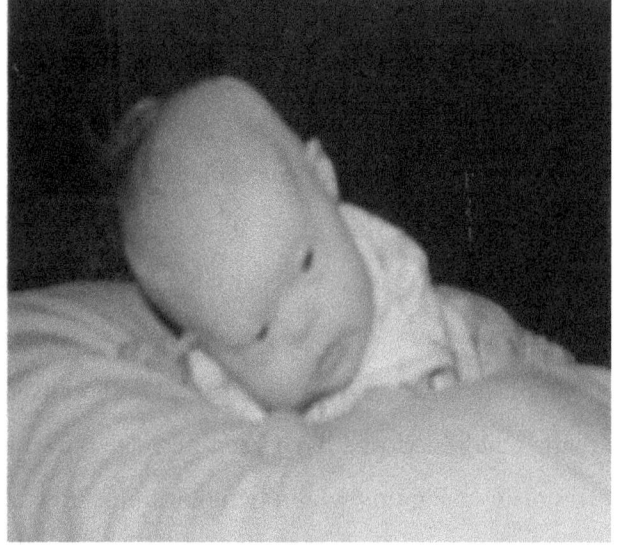

First Birthday

Birthdays are always special at our house, but first birthdays seem to be a big celebration. Probably more for the adults than the kids, because we're thinking things like "Hurrah, we made it through the first year" or "Hurrah, now we'll get more sleep." Lisa's birthday was no exception. Many invitations were sent out ahead of time, and grandparents, aunts, uncles, cousins and friends all came down to celebrate with us.

Before her first birthday, we had been practicing blowing out the candle. I really don't know how much time was spent on this activity, but it wasn't really much help for Lisa. If I remember correctly, she leaned too close to the lit candle and almost singed her eyebrows. Most of the time, her technique of blowing was more of an inhale rather than an exhale. Consequently, the lit wick barely wavered. That was also when we discovered that she didn't blow straight out, but she blew downward. Now we had to figure out the placement of the cake and candle for her to be successful. When she finally did snuff the candle out, it was with the help of a cousin. The traditional re-try was quickly waved, because Lisa seemed to be more interested in eating the cake instead of blowing out the candles. What was our first clue? Lisa had grabbed a fistful of cake and frosting as quickly as we could say "Happy Birthday."

The cake was our traditional angel food cake with sticky, white-peaked frosting. It tastes great, but clean up is horrible. Lisa was given a piece of cake, to be eaten as finger food. She had really gotten pretty limber with her fingers, and practiced what we'd been teaching her, the pincer[7] grasp. That meant she used her thumb and index finger to pick up objects. At one time, she used her palm to grab objects then later on moved to using the whole thumb and several fingers to do so. Now she was up to using the tips of her thumb and finger more often than anything. Picking up blocks was part of her practice time, but food was more fun because the reward was getting to eat it. And eating was one of Lisa's most favorite things to do.

Getting it out of her hair later was a mess but it was still worth it, watching her take a bite, smile because of the sweetness she was enjoying, followed by her putting her hands to her head and hair, for whatever reason. The ice cream was a little messy, too. And even though she could use a spoon, she used her fingers to try and pick up the cold and slippery ice cream. Pincer grasp doesn't work to well with ice cream. Talk about a drippy, sticky mess. But if you could judge the quality of a food by looking at the amount of mess on and around Lisa, it must have been great.

Presents for Lisa varied from fun to functional to educational. A standard toy for all my kids, usually from one of their aunts who was trying to be funny, was a toy drum. Lisa was no exception. Now, drums in general are noisy, and for some reason they sound like the top is made out of tin. Their rat-a-tat-tat is enough to drive anyone crazy. But Lisa loved it. She could sit down on the floor with her legs wrapped around the drum, with a drumstick in each hand, and pound on it to her hearts' content. I could list a lot of skills she was using, and I wasn't going to discourage any of it. It was the same attitude we had with most of her toys and activities. We gave her something educational her first year, and for many years to follow. I finally realized I had a mind-set of always educating her, and decided she needed to have a toy she could just have fun with. And I realized that anything fun could also be educational. Take a box. Kids usually like playing with the box as much as some of the toys that were in the box. You can talk about color, shape, size (little to big) put things in the box, under or behind it, make different shaped holes to drop different shaped items in it, and so on. Having a kid can really bring out a parent's creativity.

Lisa's first birthday was a milestone for all of us. We had welcomed a fourth child into our family and we all adjusted. I think after two or three, it just doesn't matter how many children are underfoot. The siblings learned to share and help, and hopefully be better adults for having the experience of having a sister with Down syndrome. I can't speak for Lisa's Dad, but I know I have learned patience by having Lisa in my life. After I had our third child, I wondered if I would ever be a patient person again. He was our busy beaver, always on the go, into everything and anything. Later on, during his grade school years, he was diagnosed with ADHD, attention deficit hyperactivity disorder, but up until the age of two, things were tough for both him and I. Many times I would wonder about my parenting skills, but I definitely knew I needed help with my patience. I prayed to God for patience, and I believe He sent Lisa to me, so I could learn to have the patience needed to raise Lisa.

Lisa's first birthday had me saying a prayer of thanksgiving for having her as a part of this family. She had recently undergone a heart catherization and we received the news that heart surgery was not necessary at that time. I was thankful for being her parent, and experiencing all the unique things that go along with being a parent of a child with a disability. I wouldn't have traded where I was for anything. At the end of Lisa's birthday party and after all the relatives had gone and our children were in bed, I had time to really reflect on Lisa, how she was doing, and how we, as a family, were doing. Tears of sadness were mixed with tears of joy. Joy because Lisa was able to celebrate her first birthday; that she was still with us and there was hope for her success; the sadness because of all the time I had spent feeling scared, worried or uncertain. All my questions and fears turned into looking for answers and hope. Hope for her future.

Birthdays are Times for Gratitude

Whenever I think of my children's upcoming birthdays, I experience a roller coaster of emotions. I hate to see the oldest observe another birthday, for that means I am also getting older. That's somewhat disturbing. The next two, both boys, seem to enjoy birthday celebrations, especially during their teen years. The popular gift item for them was money, and that depressed me. I always thought money seemed so impersonal, and as their mother I should know what they liked or wanted, but when they asked for money they got it, because that was safe and easy to give.

With Lisa's birthdays, I experience happiness, sadness, helplessness, concern and love. There was a time when I was unsure of my true feelings for Lisa, but I can look at her now and know that I love her unconditionally. I have accepted her as she is, knowing that her Down syndrome is only an added feature of her entire personality.

I remember reminiscing about the first years of Lisa's life, and I began to think out loud about how to tell others of my mixed feelings. It's hard to describe how you can love your child, and still be sad, or work hard for her to be independent, yet worry about her future on her own. I wrote the following poem when Lisa was almost seven, shortly after hearing about an acquaintance who gave birth to a child with serious physical and mental problems. I sat down to sort out my feelings about Lisa, and realized how capable she really was. I knew I could be proud of her, just as all parents are proud of their children.

Mountains to Climb

Several years ago our "little Lisa" was born,
Changing hopes and dreams,
'cause she's not of the 'norm'.
Her birth brought happiness….and tears,
Lost hope for the future, and many new fears.

How could we cope, how could this be?
We wanted the best that she could be.
And now we know this still can be true,
Though we've had to adjust a dream or two.
We've gone through many good and bad times;
Many roads to travel, many mountains to climb.

Her first ear infection made the ER's day.
Her first surgery took my sleep away.
Her first rollover from front to back,
Had us all on the floor where we could clap.

She made some slow but steady strides,
Like sitting, crawling, walking
and piggyback rides.
I look at her now and wonder about us.
We were mad, scared, uncertain.
Oh, why all the fuss?

Her achievements are many,
we're as proud as can be.
She seems just---SO NORMAL;
did we doubt it could be?

I have faith in the present
and the future holds hope,
That she will live with society
and our family can cope…
With the questions, the problems,
the hopes and fears,
That will be with us daily
and all through the years.

I thank God that we have her,
and all she can do.
She has shown us that life
need not always be blue;
Behind the dark clouds…a silver lining or two,
By how we adjust to the different and new.

Crawling

Lisa started off pretty much on track for the gross motor skills, such as rolling over, sitting and crawling. Some of her tactics to do these skills were rather unorthodox, but she still accomplished those milestones within the normal timeline. Once she learned to roll over, she was able to travel from room to room, even through some doorways. Sometimes she'd get stuck with her legs straddling the door jam, and then would have to wait patiently until someone could help her. She rolled around for quite awhile, until she felt comfortable with crawling. Her style of crawling was like an Army crawl, where you are in a prone position then up on your forearms, pulling your body weight without the help of your knees, legs or feet. She looked very uncomfortable because of her style, but she was able to get into more things faster with crawling. Even though she was standing up with help just before her first birthday, she chose to crawl another year before finally walking. Probably because she felt safer, being closer to the floor with crawling.

Her very first type of crawling was more of a pulling. She would remain on her stomach, with one knee flexed under her, while the other was as straight as a board. She also used one arm to pull herself across the floor, while the other arm looked like a directional device. This arm was more out front, maybe for balance, while the arm she pulled with was almost under her upper torso. With one arm out in front, she could clear a path through the toys strewn about, all the way across a large room. Of course, the wood or tile floors were easier for her to move on, but she didn't let carpet slow her down any. She was a real go-getter, especially when she found out there was more to see off her blanket than she realized.

When she first got up on all fours, it was with the help of the physical therapist. We would actually bend her knees, and then hold them in place while we lifted her upper torso. This way, she could then support herself with her hands while maintaining stiff arms. There she would stay in that position while we slowly and gently rocked her forward and backwards, trying to encourage this traditional four-point stance. In order to keep her knees under her, we had to brace her feet and keep her knees flexed. At the same time, we had to control her upper torso. In doing it this way, she wouldn't buckle under or suddenly lunge forward. Some days, depending on how cooperative she was, it went very well. Other days it almost took two people to keep her and all her body parts in alignment. In the beginning of getting her to a hands and knees position, we started by positioning her on her elbows or forearms and her knees. This encouraged her to be on her knees, but gave her arms a rest. I tried doing this myself, and realized the strain on the back and neck was too much for me. I thought that being up on my hands and knees was definitely easier. I'm sure it must have strengthened those muscles in Lisa's back and neck, so it was beneficial for her.

When she finally maintained the four-point position on her own, she began to move forward, again with help at first. One arm, opposite leg; again and again. I guess it was considered patterning in a sense, though we were just trying to encourage Lisa to do this on her own. Years ago, patterning was a passive form of therapy, meaning someone else did all the work for that person, moving the arms and legs over and over. The theory, when treating a child or an adult with a brain injury, was the undamaged sections of the brain would develop the ability to perform the functions. Well, I never thought of Lisa having "brain damage." She was just someone with an extra chromosome. And if she was considered to have brain damage because of her diagnosis, how could she have any undamaged areas, because Down syndrome affected every cell in her body. I did *not* believe she was damaged. I believed and acted on the fact that what Lisa needed was encouragement with activities that a normal infant would instinctively do, which in turn would improve Lisa's abilities.

One of Lisa's obstacles with learning to crawl was her dresses. I outfitted her with a variety of clothing, but mainly dresses because she had heaps of them. Having an older sister and female cousins was always good in having an ample amount of clothes to choose from. I also wanted her to look cute, which she did, and pretty dresses just added to her adorability. The problem was how they hung down on the floor while crawling, right at the knees. As she moved her knees forward, she would invariably catch the hem of the dress. That first knee forward would not be as disastrous as the second one. The body couldn't shift forward because the knee on the dress held it back. Then when the other knee came forward, it threw her off balance. That's when she would plunge face first to the floor. She soon learned that this was not what she wanted to continue doing. Besides, it didn't get her very far very fast.

Lisa quickly figured out how to avoid the dresses by getting up off her knees while she crawled. Her crawling technique changed from hands and knees to hands and feet, yes, feet. Who knew that she was already a pro in Yoga, doing the traditional "Downward-facing Dog Pose" without any problems! She was able to maintain this position, with her bottom up in the air, and crawl around. It was not all the time, but when she caught her dress with a knee, it was like an immediate reaction to then go to the hands and feet position. She managed pretty well, and I am sure it strengthened lots of muscles in the process. This was also a handy way to avoid the toys on the floor without having to go around them. She just got into the hands and feet position and "crawled" right over them. She had several different styles of crawling, so I attribute this to why she crawled for so long.

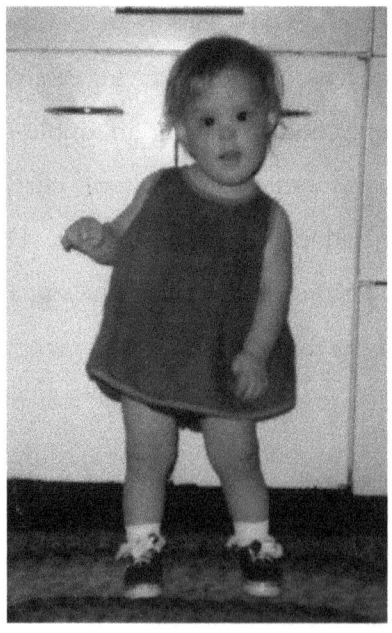

Walking

When would Lisa finally start to walk on her own? No one knew, but there was much speculation. And, until it actually happened, all bets were off. The teacher had been telling me for months, well, actually for a year, that Lisa would walk soon. It was always, "Next week, I know she'll be walking." I believed this teacher, but somebody forgot to tell Lisa.

Lisa managed to meet all the usual progressive milestones, such as rolling over, sitting alone and crawling. Her crawling was unconventional, even though we tried to pattern Lisa to a four-point (hands and knees) crawl. She pulled herself in such an unorthodox way by positioning herself on her stomach and her arms folded under her upper torso. She let one leg remain straight, pulled with her arms, and pushed with the other leg that was flexed. The straight leg simply followed along. Once in awhile, she would actually get up on that flexed knee and even more rarely, on both knees. If she did succeed in being up on all fours it didn't last, and just as quickly the front of her body would be next to the ground, with her arms trapped underneath. I was unable to be of any help to her to figure out the quandary at hand. There she would stay, with her head resting on the floor, her legs bent in a 90-degree angle at the knees and her bottom pointing up in the air. She didn't move very well in this position.

After months of slow progression in crawling, she finally began to stand by furniture, not daring to move a single muscle probably for fear of falling. But she did fall; quite often. To cushion the falls, I would arrange various blankets and pillows around her immediate fall area. At first, the pillows seemed to divert her attention, and she gingerly tried to reach for these brightly colored distractions. She soon learned if she reached out she fell, so she limited her reaching as much as possible. I don't know if the bumper blankets did much in the way of protection, for she still had many bruises to show for her wobbly state. I do know it was short lived, as the blankets got in the way once she began to take those ever-so-slightly small steps.

I removed the barrier, and encouraged her to step forward by placing a favorite toy just out of her reach on the couch or table where she was anchored. Once again Lisa's favorite toy, the porcupine, helped her during her beginning stages of walking. I've never seen an orange porcupine, but nevertheless, this toy attracted Lisa the most, probably because of the color and texture. Those bristly appendages must have felt good across her sensitive hands and face, for she would laugh and giggle each time we massaged her with this toy. This favorite toy was the enticement she needed to try moving her feet forward or sideways towards the object.

The teacher who came to our house twice a week was encouraged by Lisa's progress, always commenting on how good she was doing each time we met for a session. Even more surprised was the Physical therapist who visited less often, and saw vast improvements when she came to work with Lisa. The two teachers began to say things like "It won't be long now, and she'll take off," or "You'd better start childproofing your house; she'll be into everything soon." Didn't they realize Lisa was already doing quite well getting into things without walking? But, I encouraged her progress, looking to the day when I would no longer have to carry her around. That day was still a long way off. Lisa did not improve in leaps and bounds, nor did she want to leap or bound. She was content to sit in one place, checking out the living room décor or scoot awkwardly towards her targeted object. Nevertheless, we continued to encourage independent standing and walking. I have pictures of Lisa standing in front of our kitchen cupboards, seemingly very pleased with her feat. The photos clearly do not show the reason for her smile. She did not have to stand on her own, but was propped in such a way that she could use the cupboards as her back support. She thought she was hot stuff, which shows in her wily grin.

Lisa finally began to maneuver on her own, after almost a year of encouragement. She took little steps at first, timidly and carefully. The worst thing she could do was fall, because she had such a difficult time trying to stand up again. She did master the standing up skillfully, but in a somewhat unusual way. As she sat on the floor, she straightened out her legs in front of her, and in some distorted fashion, using her hands and arms, pushed herself to her feet, while never once bending at the knees. Her upper body would lean forward and the strength she acquired in her arms was enough to complete this task. I guess all the GI-style crawling did her some good. If she couldn't stand back up, she would have to sit after a fall until someone could pick her up, place her flatly on her feet and give a small, encouraging nudge to try walking again. At the age of two, Lisa was walking on her own accord, though ever so carefully. She also had a vision problem that hindered her walking. She could not look down to see the floor very well. We did not know this right away, but I always wondered what fascinated her so much that she would constantly look down at her feet and cautiously step forward as if walking off a plank. It was only later, after she had glasses, that I saw her pick up speed, take chances on small inclines and steps as well as lifting one leg up to step over an obstacle in her way.

As far as carrying her, I still did quite a bit of that. It's not that she wasn't capable of walking, but it was simply a matter of time. Her idea of walking fast was to swing her arms as fast as she could while her pace remained the same. I began to tire of waiting for her, and tired of repeating the words "Hurry up." I knew I had to let her walk as much as possible, for her sake, but once in awhile, no actually a lot in the beginning, I would pick her up and carry her. It was on the pretense of wiping her nose or brushing the hair from her face. But once in my arms, I quickly moved her with me to our destination. I may have delayed her independence with walking, yet at the time I could rationalize this action to save my sanity. I never did write down an official date for her walking debut, as I couldn't decide if there ever was a specific date. We had worked on it for many, many months and her progress was not an overnight success. My other children have that space filled in with the day and month they took off walking on their own. With Lisa, I put down the year 1982.

Sitting and Chairs

Lisa has never been a real active person, choosing to sit instead of moving about. It's just where and how she sat that was a problem. When she was a baby, she sat just fine on the floor on a blanket and didn't move much. This lasted until she learned to crawl, when the limitations of the blanket area were much too confining. I would try to keep her on that blanket with toys to hold her interest, but she was curious enough to venture off on an exploration of whatever room we were in. Countless times I would pick her up or playfully "drag" her back to the blanket, only to do it over again and again. Secretly though, I was pleased with her activity, rationalizing all the plusses of her mobility. She was curious, she was learning skills to move on her own, she had the initiative to do this, and she had a determination or stubbornness to repeat this despite continued efforts on my part to keep her on the blanket. She was beginning to be her own person, to think for herself and to be more mobile. Who was I to contain that? I would never want to buy a playpen, because I believed exploration was good. It just kept me busy, even though she didn't move very fast or very far.

As Lisa got a little older, learning to sit for extended periods was important, like in her high chair, at church or in school. Well, two out of three wasn't too bad. Sitting in church was pretty good, especially if there was food to keep her busy. Yes, food in church. I believe this is almost unheard of in some churches. But, with marshmallows, small crackers or cheerios, Lisa was content and we were able to stay in church for the entire service. The biggest obstacle with the food was trying to keep her two older brothers from eating what was to be just for Lisa. They were old enough to know better, but they figured if she could eat in church, they could, too. Our other option was the cry room, which I figured should only be used if the baby or child was crying. Otherwise, for my children, the cry room wasn't an option. So food was the method of appeasement for Lisa. This was probably not a good way to encourage positive behavior with Lisa, even if it did work, as people with Down syndrome tend to be overweight. But, at her young age, she was actually a lightweight, so I wasn't too concerned about her weight at the time.

Sitting in a high chair wasn't too difficult for Lisa, because food was involved and she loved to eat. The worst time for sitting in the high chair was when Lisa was learning to feed herself. That's when we chose the finger foods over items like gelatin, soups or her very favorite, mashed potatoes. Even when she learned to use a spoon, it was still rather messy with these foods. And if any of these slick foods got on the seat, she would slip around a lot in her high chair. She never really fit well in the seat, even when we tried several different adaptations. At first, we tried to use a towel to tie her in place. This still left a lot of room on either side, so a rolled towel on either side was also used to keep her from leaning too far either way. She still slipped down in her seat, and many times ended up with the tied towel up under her arm pits and her legs dangling out front with no place to rest them. You have to remember, Lisa was short, which caused her to have trouble reaching the footrest of the high chair. Even in the suspended position, she could just barely touch the footrest with her toes. We even tried building up the footrest by adding a block of wood. This didn't stay in place very good, and ended up being more trouble than it was worth. She spent a lot of time with her feet in the air with no support, whether she was dangling or not.

This particular problem, having legs too short, carried over into the school setting. Let me explain about the preschool cube chair with two different seat levels. If the chair is placed one way, the seat is molded to be higher; turn it over and the seat is molded into a much lower setting. It was also difficult to add a footrest to these cube chairs. For that reason, Lisa spent a lot of time swinging her feet, as she could not touch the floor with either molded seat she sat in. If not swinging her feet, she would sit crossways in the cube chair, with her head and arms over one armrest, and her legs, still dangling, over the other side. It did not look like a comfortable position, and was definitely not very ladylike. I was embarrassed on the days I'd come to visit the classroom and realize that I had outfitted Lisa in a dress. Not a pretty sight when she was in her relaxed position in the cube chair.

Usually Lisa did her patented "sitting" technique when the low seat was close to the floor, and the armrests were higher, making the sides very tall. Lisa would put her arms on the high sides and lift herself up. Consequently, her bottom was suspended, not touching the chair seat. She could also swing side to side if she chose to do so. If the chair was flipped and the seat was high, which had the armrests at a minimum height, she could still use her technique, but she couldn't swing with the short armrests and still her feet never touched the floor. For entertainment in this position, she would bend her knees and have her feet were under the seat, like they were trying to grab hold from underneath. Most of the time, this was short-lived because it threw her off balance, and she'd topple forward, face first, and the cube chair ended up on top of her. The other chair option was a small wooden one that sat higher than a cube chair, and definitely had to have a footrest. There was always one such chair with a large cardboard building block attached to the two front legs with masking or duct tape. One of the problems with this chair was there were no sides or arm rests for support. One slight movement and Lisa was off the side and on the floor. (A lot of times by choice, I think.)

For Lisa, chairs never fit her body type, but she still learned a combination of ways to sit. I think her favorite kind of chair was the wheelchairs that other children in the classes had to use. If these students ever spent classroom time out of their chair for a change of position, you could always find Lisa in or near the wheelchairs. She did well climbing up in them, even when they rolled off in another direction as if in retreat from her. Once in a chair, she would just sit. The chair was always too big for her, but here she would sit holding onto the armrests, and look straight ahead with a smug look on her face. She kept a firm grip, knowing someone would come along soon to get her out. When she learned how to buckle the belt, it took a little more effort from the classroom adults to get her out. Some wheelchairs had a high back that also had the shoulder and chest straps. Lisa was very capable of slipping her arms and chest through the appropriate straps, and getting everything buckled and pulled tight. So, even though she shouldn't be doing this, I felt pretty good about how she could maneuver into the chair and work the straps without help. My thought was that she was using her cognitive skills to analyze and solve the problem and she figured out how to get safely and securely in the chair. The teachers had a different view.

To try and give Lisa some positive encouragement, the teachers allowed Lisa the opportunity to be around the wheelchairs when it was appropriate, not just when Lisa wanted to get away from classroom activities. Lisa was given the privilege of helping the student who was in the wheelchair. She would push the wheelchair on occasion, for a short distance, and always with teacher supervision. I don't believe this lasted very long, for several reasons. Lisa's attention span was brief, especially when it was something the teachers or other adults wanted her to do. And, she became adamantly disinterested when she found out that pushing a wheelchair was WORK.

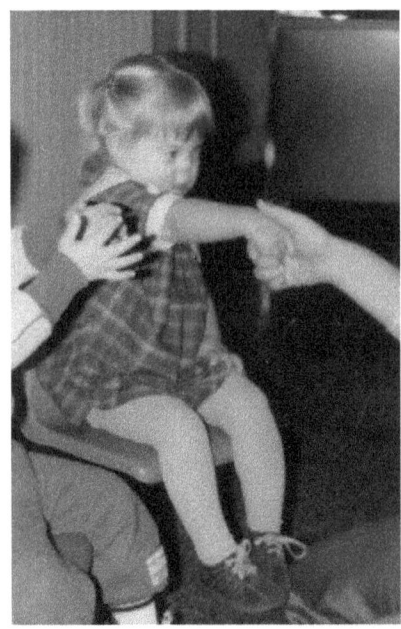

Vision

We don't know an exact date that Lisa began to walk, so that line item in the baby book is vague. I remember that it was just around her first birthday when she could stand and support herself well enough to take a step or two, but she really didn't walk by her first birthday. Her physical therapist saw her weekly at first, then twice a month later on, and would say "Any day now. She'll walk on her own." I think I heard that for almost a year, and began to wonder whether she ever really would walk on her own. She was able to walk holding onto someone's hands, two hands at first, then down to just holding on to one hand. But, she just seemed so unsure of herself and I couldn't figure out why.

When she finally did walk on her own, she seemed to fall a lot, but it looked liked she might have planned it that way. Usually she'd just plop down after a few steps, or hang onto a table, chair or wall. Even when holding onto furniture, she seemed unsteady and wasn't able to reach for an object appropriately. I just figured her unsteadiness caused her arm to bob around, until she could steady herself to grab the object she was reaching for. We finally thought that something more might be wrong when she would try to walk through a doorway, stop, look ahead as if deciding where to walk and then proceed cautiously through the doorway. We found out later that the eye doctor said she was probably seeing double, and she was hesitant to choose which door she should walk through. I'd bet if she chose the wrong one, she would have ended up walking into a wall instead. Glad she had enough sense to be cautious. Her eyesight had probably been bad from birth, but we didn't notice because her activities were always at close range.

The first visit to the eye doctor was interesting, because they couldn't do a normal chart exam. You know, where the biggest letters are at the top and each line below was somewhat smaller. If she could read, she probably still couldn't see that top line from 10 feet out. And even when she was older and COULD read letters, most of the time she didn't want to read them out loud or the examiner wasn't sure of her answers, as she was very soft spoken. Most of the time the results were not exact.

At the first visit, I had to hold her in my lap while they did an examination. This was also one of the times I actually paid more attention to the examiner than to what Lisa was doing. Since then, I have chosen eye doctors for Lisa on the basis of a first visit, evaluating the receptionist, the exam and the doctor. My system of deciding included watching how the staff treated her, talked to her and handled her. If they were hesitant, standoffish or rude, I may have decided I would not come back. But, most of the different eye doctors she has seen were pretty good. I only remember one time during an eye exam with Lisa, I thought that maybe we wouldn't be back to that eye doctor. He was in a hurry with the exam, not giving her time to answer, and had very little patience in waiting for her to reply with an answer when he would ask questions like "Is number one better, or is number two better?" I might have even given the eye doctors a few pointers in working with Lisa, and conceded to let them have another try with Lisa before deciding they couldn't give Lisa what I thought was the best care possible. I'm really not that tough on the professionals, no matter what you've heard.

When Lisa was able to talk and be understood, they tried to use the preschool eye test. This test used capital letter E that pointed towards certain pictures. This was not too successful at first, because the pictures were a girl, boy, bird and bunny. Three out of four had the beginning sound of the letter B, and sometimes all we got out of her was a B sound. Subsequently, we relied on hand signals, such as flapping wings for bird and hopping movement for bunny. The tester still had trouble deciphering the answer. And when they would ask her "Did you say boy?," that just encouraged a yes answer from Lisa, but it may not have been HER answer.

We also tried to have her use a card that had a letter E on it, and have her turn it in the same direction as the E that was pointing on the test wall. And we tried having duplicate pictures of each near her so she could point to the correct one she was seeing on the wall. I'm still not sure she got the best visual correction this way, but they tried. Probably the closest they got was by looking into her eyes with whatever equipment they used to see whatever they look at, and then decide how poor Lisa's vision was.

Her first pair of glasses was small and had thick lenses. I still have them saved away with her countless baby mementos. The temples had spring-hinges and the ends of the temples wrapped around her ears. There was also a small nose bridge with moveable nose guards. The hinged temples were a feature we chose, which was a blessing to have. She tried to bend them more than normal, but those hinges held firm. She didn't really ever try to take them off, probably because the glasses helped her to see. It's like when my husband got glasses the first time, long after we were married, he said he could finally see the leaves on the trees. In Lisa's case, with glasses, it was probably then possible for her to see the trees.

She had a major problem keeping the glasses up on her face. Her nose wasn't much larger than a flat half-inch button and no matter what kind of nose pads we used, the glasses slipped. A substitute kind of pad was cushiony on one side, and when you peeled off the back piece of protective covering, it was able to stick to whatever nose pads came with the glasses. Those pads were a real mess when they got wet and Lisa's nose, as small as it was, would get sweaty a lot. The pads crumbled or wouldn't stick, so we replaced them a lot. I bought different sized, experimenting with cutting different shapes that would most benefit Lisa and her tiny nose. The worst thing they did was attract more attention to her, because the pads were obviously larger than necessary and Lisa's eyes would focus on them, making her look cross-eyed. Keeping her glasses on was a never-ending battle.

Those spring-hinged temples wrapped so far around her ears that the tips showed up in pictures near her jaw line, directly under the ear lobes, and it looked like she was wearing earrings. She also wore a sports band around the back of her head when she first got her glasses. That band was placed under her hair and as a result, it didn't look too awfully bad, but it constantly got tangled in her long hair. Tangles and long hair made it almost impossible to undo without some crying. I was glad when we could do away with the strap. The nose guards on the glasses had improved enough that the substance they used seemed to hold the glasses in place fairly well. We still have some classic pictures of Lisa's glasses down on the tip of her nose, and she's peering over the top rim of the glasses. She either looks very important, like those people who use the ½ size "cheater" glasses for reading, or she looks like an old granny. I voted for the first description, important.

Her vision seemed to waver with the kind of work she was doing at the time, close up verses distant. She also had a problem with night blindness and depth perception. I suppose the depth perception was part of her problem when she was learning to walk. Looking down is a part of walking, and if she couldn't judge the distance, walking could have been confusing with each step. The night blindness bothered her most when she would be outside at night with very little light. Still today, Lisa takes each step very cautiously and usually needs someone's hand to feel comfortable. Walking down steps at night is difficult for her, too. Trick or treating in the neighborhood was scary for her; all those steps up to people's front doors were taken slow and deliberately measured.

More recently, we have noticed problems in places where there are steps that are lit up in the dark, such as in a movie theater. The top and bottom steps are illuminated in red, while the others are white in color. Either the color or position of the step is a problem for her, because she cannot see to go up or down very well without physical help. And turning on the lights in a theater is just not realistic. What we did was cope, modify, and work towards helping her through those difficult situations. A small flashlight worked best in most situations. A helping hand was and is always a steady support. And, telling her what is coming next on whatever surface she's walking on helps her to be a little sure of her stride. It sometimes felt like we were still taking baby steps, but Lisa usually gets where she needs to be. We can now see the positive results of all the efforts.

Dr. Non-believer

I had some trouble after Lisa's birth, trying to believe that she really did have Down syndrome. And until I had positive proof, mainly the chromosome report, I kept hoping the doctors were wrong. Once I had the results in black and white, I was able to get past it, and begin to focus on what's important for Lisa and her future. Interestingly, several years later, I had to convince a doctor that she truly did have Down syndrome!

It all started when Lisa had an appointment with a state clinic program that did exams for children with disabilities. In Lisa's case, they were not following her Down syndrome diagnosis, but her heart condition. There were doctors from a large hospital who came to smaller communities across the state, setting up specific days and times for many children to be seen. As far as I remember, there was no cost or maybe a minimal cost, depending on income. Doctors from our local clinics were also involved, but I don't remember if Lisa was ever seen by her own doctor on her visits to these this special medical clinics.

Lisa's second or third visit to this health program was with an older doctor who had a private practice in our town. I remember this doctor had seen her before at one of the clinics, because in the typed report he made comments about Lisa, her "definite diagnosis of Down Syndrome," and listed the physical features he saw. He mentioned things like the sloping forehead, flat nose and low-set ears. I wondered if he thought he was telling us something we didn't already know. We knew she had these features, and we knew what they meant, Down syndrome. I was not impressed with the redundancy, especially when I thought this was to be a heart evaluation.

The next time this doctor saw her at a follow-up clinic, it seemed like he had never examined her before. And it sounded like he was retracting his earlier diagnosis, specifically the fact that she had Down syndrome. Lisa was walking by this time, though not real well. But, her speech was pretty good, especially for someone who was just a little over two years old and had Down syndrome. Lisa was talking about the picture on the wall in the office we were in, pointing and identifying many objects in the artwork. Of course, I encouraged this verbal interaction, and would ask her questions about the different things she pointed to. If she said cow, I would continue with "What does the cow say? What do we get from the cow that we drink? What does the cow eat?" and so on. She could identify a lot of objects and answered most questions appropriately. She was forming complete sentences and putting a little inflection in her tone of voice. A lot of this was because of our encouragement at home, and the help we received from her homebound and speech teachers. This early schooling had been very beneficial to her and us. We were taught how to help her to learn.

When the doctor walked in and heard Lisa talking, he started questioning the diagnosis of Down syndrome, especially the fact that it was Trisomy 21, one of the most common types of Down syndrome. The two other less common types are called Mosaic and Translocation. Children with these types of Down syndrome may be considered higher functioning intellectually than an individual with the Trisomy 21 type. I told the doctor that Lisa had the chromosome tests done at birth and it was definitely Trisomy 21. I also brought it to his attention that his first evaluation of her was definitely Trisomy 21. At that first visit he had with Lisa, when she was just a baby, I specifically remembered that at the end of his evaluation, he recommended that we just take her home. He said the early childhood programs were just a waste of time, and Lisa would learn later on her own but not to expect much. She'd never read, tell time, and yes, I think he even said she'd never talk very well, if at all. But now, seeing her and hearing her speaking so well at such a young age, he would not hear of such talk or acknowledge that he had ever said any of those things.

I told the doctor how we had been working with her, what kinds of activities we were doing and Lisa's successes. The doctor wouldn't listen to this explanation. In fact, he still insisted that any early intervention was useless. He remarked that children with Down syndrome would learn at their own pace, in their own time. He did not support any kind of special education at such a young age. He said they would start school at the age of seven or eight and do just fine. I tried to disagree but kept thinking, "How could I change his mind, to see what we've seen, to know that the earlier the help the better prepared she would be?" I told him I would send a copy of the chromosome report if he wanted. I did send this report, but Lisa did not see him after that last encounter. However, when Lisa had her yearly evaluation, before going into a kindergarten-age setting, I knew I had MY proof on the positive effects of early childhood education for children with disabilities. Lisa had scored extremely high on the tests they do before entering kindergarten; so high that her test results showed she did not qualify for special education. It didn't matter that she had Down syndrome; she didn't qualify. The administration was pleasantly surprised, yet in a sticky situation. We all knew and agreed Lisa still needed a support system, even with her high scores. She probably achieved such success because of her early education and we wanted that to continue. As a group, the special education staff, as well as Lisa's Dad and I, decided Lisa would need more than a regular kindergarten classroom could provide. If she were placed in a regular kindergarten without supports, our fear was she would just be left behind, in the dust, if she were in a classroom with 25-30 other children and one teacher. But in order to get the extra help she needed, we had to write in the rationale. And so, in the space provided for "OTHER," since she didn't qualify according to tests results, we wrote: Due to her congenital diagnosis of Down syndrome, she will need continued support in her academics.

We also decided not to give her a break in her education, but instead doubled up on her schooling. She enjoyed school and never seemed stressed by it. For those reasons, we agreed to have her attend full days as a kindergartener. But, it was split in an unusual way. You must remember this was during a time when no school offered a full-day kindergarten class. In Lisa's situation, she would spend her mornings in a program through the special educational department, with part of that time in a regular kindergarten setting in that same building as the special ed program. After that morning program, she went by bus to a daycare school that also had a kindergarten-age group, which continued her kindergarten studies. This gave her twice the amount of education and stimulation to enhance her learning. She had always been in some kind of school program, and she seemed to thrive on it, so why give her a break now. In fact, when she had a two-week break before and after the summer school programs, she seemed lost. It was almost like a punishment NOT to send her to school. At the beginning of each school year, she would get so excited about starting back, that her questions day after day were about when she would be going back to school. I was glad to get her back in the school setting after every vacation break, because I knew I couldn't give her the intense, positive stimulation she needed to continue learning.

When I got a copy of the kindergarten evaluation with the initial response being she didn't qualify for special services due to her high score, I sent a copy to the doctor who had such a difficult time believing early education would do her any good at such an early age. It was kind of like an "I told you so," which may not have been a nice way for me to react but I sent it anyway. I was a strong believer in early education, and this just confirmed for me what could be accomplished. If I could change that one doctor's mind, it just might influence many others he comes in contact with. Who knows!

Potty Training

Spring fever means different things to different people. When my kids were little, spring meant dragging out the shorts and sandals, dressing less, getting outside more. It also meant training time; potty training, that is. After going through this process with three kids, you'd think I'd know better, but I made the same mistakes again. With Lisa, I definitely started too soon.

As soon as she was standing on her own, I got the spring "training" fever. I found all the old training pants, and salvaged the ones I could. These were the basic white, elastic waist, vented sides and triple thickness middle/center panel. I also invested in some new ones that looked more "girly," and I bought many plastic pants. Does anyone even use those anymore? You know, when you used cloth diapers, you also had to use the plastic pants for protection. Well, I knew that using these plastic pants with the training pants defeated the "training" somewhat, but my rationale seemed right to me. I didn't want her to have her outer pants, like her shorts, get wet nor did I want to have wet hands every time I picked her up. The plastic protected both of us. So at first, I used th0se plastic pants.

I thought when Lisa could stand by herself, gravity would play a part in her awareness of what was going on. Well, she still sat more than she stood, so I had a lot of wet underpants, and when she was without the plastic pants, a lot of wet spots on the carpet. I spent quite a bit of time running her to the bathroom, half the time when it was already too late. One of my dresser drawers in our bedroom housed her changes of slacks, underwear and plastic pants, to save me from running upstairs to her room all day long. The reason for the use of pull up cloth pants and plastic pants instead of a diaper was for her to someday be able to take them on and off by herself. I'm not sure she ever did this much, because even after she was "potty trained," I would help her expedite the process of taking them off. She moved so slowly!

Now, I got to wondering about this training business. Who was suppose to be getting trained, her or me? I was trained to check her often and take her to the bathroom at the slightest hint of her having to go. After the first go 'round in the spring and summer months, she was on a fairly regular schedule, which helped her to have less accidents. Of course, adding extra fluids before a nap or taking longer to shop at the store and missing a potty break could easily disrupt it.

Once the plastic pants were off, usually after a long string of successful days, it was still a long time before Lisa was truly dry all the time. Winter made things a little more difficult. More clothes and colder legs chapped from the wetness and more accidents, to name a few. I'm sure everyone was wondering about my state of mind, like why did I think she could be trained so young? My worry was she would be going to school packing a lunch bag and a diaper bag. As it was, when she was 3, and started in the Toddler program, we would pack extra clothes and underwear. I will admit now that I started the process too soon and it took forever. But she started kindergarten with no extra bags of anything. Hurrah!

Maybe I should have sent some extra changes of clothing even before that point in time, because there were times when I think it would have saved me a trip to school. One summer day, while she was attending the 8-week summer program, I got a call from the school nurse. She quickly identified herself and said "Lisa was on the playground and had an accident." Immediately, my heart started to speed up, my ears perked up, and I asked what happened and how badly was she hurt. The nurse realized how worried I was, and said it was nothing like that. She had just wet her pants. Whew! So, I took a change of underpants and clothes for Lisa and another set of dry clothes for the school to have on hand, just in case.

When we started this project of potty training, the big question was what kind of potty-chair to use. I really liked the oval shaped ones that fix over a regular stool seat, because this was the natural place to go, and there was less mess for me to clean up. But this had its drawbacks. Lisa was too short, and she couldn't just get up on that high bathroom stool by herself. That was okay in the beginning, because I would just lift her up there. But later on, when I wanted her to be more independent, we had to buy a step stool so she could get up to the regular bathroom stool by herself. This was a sight to see. She would step up on the step stool, facing that cold, porcelain toilet. With support from the wall on the right and the sink on the left, she was able to turn around. Next, she had to pull her pants down, which took quite a balancing act. I also remember her trying to pull her pants down while still standing on the floor. Then the trick was to step up on the footstool with the slacks and underpants around her ankles. If by some feat of agility and strength she made it that far, she would next have to turn around, inch by inch, shuffling her feet through the wads of material around her ankles. She did it, but it took forever and it wasn't very safe.

At first, when I started having her sit on the attachable seat, she was not comfortable with this new view of things. I think her vision had something to do with it, because of her depth perception problem. For her to look down, from anywhere, must have been distorted and scary. As a result, I spent a lot of time with her, just holding on to her and reassuring her that she would not fall off or in the toilet.

The nice thing about this attachable seat was its portability. The handy potty seat could taken anywhere. It was better than a regular attached toilet seat rim, because you didn't usually have to hold her to keep her from falling in. Not to say she didn't fall in; she did. That's usually because the attachable seat was not properly placed, and once Lisa was on, the seat would slip off, with her bare bottom slipping down into the toilet bowl water. Boy, I never thought potty training could be so dangerous.

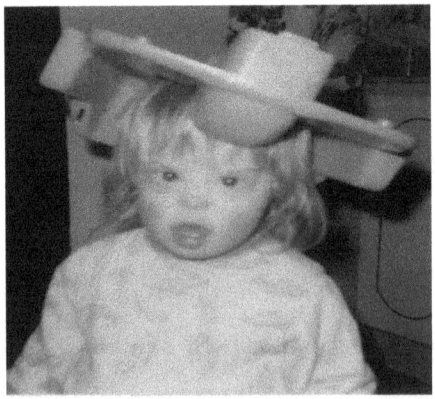

The Toddler Program

Lisa was lucky. She had two brothers and a sister to learn the basics about getting along with others. She learned how to interact, share and stand up for herself. The problem was, the only skill she carried over to her first school-based setting, the Toddler program, was being able to stand up for herself. There was very little interacting and sharing with others in the beginning. Maybe it was her age, the new setting or maybe it was the kids themselves. Whatever it was, Lisa did not do well making friends in school.

The Toddler program was geared for children aged 3-5, and set in an old school building near our home. Before entering the Toddler program, Lisa and others from birth to 3 were taught at home by a teacher who visited the individual homes once or twice a week. The Toddler program was designed to get kids out of the house, and brought them together for interaction and readiness for kindergarten. It was like a transition time between the homebound program and kindergarten.

It was a great idea, and it was here that Lisa met her first friends who ended up moving on to other grades with her for quite a few years. The beginning was rough though, trying to teach Lisa how to share and interact appropriately. But, she wasn't the only one. All these little kids were thrown together, with strange (as in unfamiliar) adults, different toys and only basic coping skills learned from their family environment.

As part of the program, parents were asked to stay through a session on a regular basis, helping out with the activities and bringing a treat for snack time. It was fun, educational and a real eye opener for me. The fun part was spending time with Lisa, the educational part was spending time with Lisa, and the eye-opening part was spending time with Lisa.

There were toys that were new and different for Lisa, and it gave her an opportunity to develop skills in a variety of ways. The same old activity on matching shapes turned into a fun new game with different puzzles and form boards available to use. Now, there were neat little cube chairs for Lisa to climb on and sit in, and like the preschool program, they also had two different seat levels. One side sat the child up pretty high, about 12' off the floor. At this level, the sides of this chair were pretty low; therefore there wasn't as much support. Lisa did okay sitting in this colorful cube chair, but again, her feet didn't touch the floor. When she used the higher seat, the staff continually tried to modify the chair by putting a large cardboard "building block" as a footrest for her. The lower seat was much closer to the floor, but not a very good position to sit at a table. In the lower position, the sides were high, which gave Lisa the stability to control her core and steady her sitting.

Lisa, like all the other children in this Toddler program, would grab their favorite toy and spend time playing alone. Having two children share a toy or having two identical toys available encouraged interaction, as did having two children sit next to each other during puzzle time and having them help each other find their puzzle pieces. Heaven forbid if one child decided to claim ownership over a toy or puzzle piece. This was when you found out just how strong-willed a child was under stress. I can still see Lisa and another child, a boy, struggling over a puzzle; neither child could withstand much physical force or they would fall over. Their verbal skills for sharing consisted of such words as "no" and "mine," as well as some unrecognizable words that sounded more like nasal squawking. Lisa's continuous, high pitched, monotone "Ahh,Ahh,Ahh" was a definite cry for help. There were winners and losers with every confrontation, and probably more diplomatically handled at school rather than at home. At home, Lisa's brothers and sister didn't really stand a chance, as Lisa was probably spoiled rotten and consequently was able to "win" every time because of it.

Learning to share is difficult, and having a disability was no excuse not to learn about sharing. The great moments came when they did actually share. I can still remember the times when Lisa thought of others and took a toy over to the boy in a wheelchair or the girl in the standing frame. I don't know what she was thinking, but she must have thought they needed a toy or companionship. Lisa was not a very outgoing or forward person, so this gesture of reaching out was amazing to see. She did like helping others, though she usually didn't instigate sharing on her own.

Keeping friends in the toddler program wasn't too difficult. Being with the same children at least twice a week got to be routine and familiarity encouraged more openness. It was kind of like with family; you could argue, fight or get mad, but you knew they would still be around. Of course, arguing, fighting or getting mad weren't appropriate in the classroom setting. In this school setting, the teachers addressed each individual incidence and handled them appropriately, depending on the offense.

I remember a specific area that was always used for time-outs.

You know, when a child gets blamed for the act, he or she needed to be removed from the situation to take time to cool off or think about what occurred and why. Also, that person needed to decide not to do it again. In fact, the standard last question was always "Will you do that again?" Now, the correct answer would be "no." But there were times when I believe Lisa said yes. I'm not sure she understood the question, or if she really believed she would repeat the act that put her in the time out area to begin with.

If it involved hitting someone who was trying to take her food, I would lay odds that yes, she would do it again. Normally, she would not even answer the question because she was distraught over actually being punished for something. She rarely did anything wrong. She was not aggressive. She was not loud. She was not outgoing. She did have classmates as friends though, with the help of teachers and other parents. Each year got a little easier for her to make friends, and the interaction helped her to know what to do when she was away from the school setting. It is difficult making friends when you're quiet and shy, but more difficult when you also have a disability, and the friends you are trying to get to know are also quiet, shy and have a disability. But, the teachers kept trying, year after year, to instill certain qualities and habits that could lead to the students making friends with others. Because really, everyone can use a friend.

Speech

Along with having a homebound teacher, Lisa was in need of a physical therapist, an occupational therapist and a speech therapist. Physical and occupational therapies helped Lisa in the area of her motor skills. The homebound teacher helped her in general, utilizing all her abilities to work towards other goals. Holding her head up led to looking around, which led to learning to reach out to touch things, which led to wanting to move towards those new things, which led to walking, which led to…well, you get the picture about building all her skills. Speech and language are learned through hearing, vision and touch, according to the National Down Syndrome Society.[8]

Children with Down syndrome may have issues with speech, in part because of the difficulties in language comprehension. And because of low muscle tone, they may not be able to physically move the tongue, lips and mouth appropriately to form the correct sounds that lead to clearer speech. Another factor that may affect learning is related to hearing, with ear infections being one of the frequent causes of hearing issues. Lisa had many ear infections, starting as early as three months of age!

The speech teacher came to the house at least twice a month. At first, we just worked on things such as noisemaking and observing her reactions. This was easy enough to do, but in the beginning I felt rather foolish. Every time Lisa made a sound, like a coo or other indistinguishable noise (excluding belching from stomach gas or flatulence) I would have to repeat the noise to her, as a way of encouraging her to continue, and do that same sound again. You know how some first-time parents do the goo, goo, ga, ga noises in an annoying, high-pitched voice; well, I may have done that a little with my other children, but usually believed in talking to them using a normal tone and real words to encourage real talk.

Now, I had to revert to this mimicking to help Lisa to talk. I figured, if this four-year college graduate, who was Lisa's teacher, said it would help, well then, I'd do just about anything. So here we were, making noises during diaper changes, before and after a bottle-feeding, (you know it's not nice to talk with your mouth full), in the stores and even in church. Church was one place that I normally wanted my kids to be seen and not heard, but not with Lisa. I encouraged her to verbalize any time, any place. I was so proud of any new sound she made, always repeating and encouraging more from her. I believe this is one of the things that helped her speech.

One of her first goals or objectives was to "vocalize when talked to." The words in quotes were taken directly from the homebound teacher's weekly notes, which included instructions for me. Believe me, this directive was not as simple as it sounds. Instructions for me were to approach Lisa when she was "babbling or in vocal play activity." I was usually holding her, so the approach was really not necessary.

Next, I was to pick her up and hold her in a face-to-face position. Okay, so now what? Once again, according to the teacher's directions, I was to "mimic her vocalizations, repeat what she babbles, encourage her to repeat back and keep repeating." For positive reinforcements, we were to say things like "Good talking," smile and bounce her. I charted everything she did, how well and how often. It was worth it; she progressed nicely.

I questioned one goal objective that stated Lisa would explore objects placed in her hands. It also encouraged bringing a toy to her face, cheeks and mouth. A final instruction was to "Help her throw or drop the object." She did so well with putting things in her mouth and throwing items that we had to have another objective for her to bring only appropriate items, such as food to her mouth and not throw toys or food.

Her speech teacher introduced another speech activity to Lisa when she was a few months older. We would put a little dab of peanut butter on the roof of her mouth, and she would try to use her tongue to get it off. I called these her tongue exercises. We would also dab peanut butter on either side of the inside of her mouth or on an upper or lower lip. Lisa really worked hard to get that peanut butter, yum, yum. I think this single exercise did a lot for Lisa's speech. She actually talked before she could walk, and it was fairly easy to understand her words.

Lisa's early years at "school" were interesting and certainly a learning experience for all of the family. All her homebound teachers explained the activities, did a run through with Lisa, and seemed to truly care about Lisa, her progress and us. One of the reasons for Lisa's success in learning has to be because of those special teachers. We were lucky to be living in Nebraska, with those caring, compassionate educators. To all of you who worked with Lisa, thank you for choosing that profession and for being a part of Lisa's life.

Medicines and Being Sick

If I had to give a prize to the one child of mine who saw the doctor the most, it would be to Lisa. Sometime, those visits were because of her heart problem, but most of the time it was for congestion or ear infections. Medically speaking, people with Down syndrome have a tendency to have Eustachian tube problems, maybe due to the fact that the ear canals are narrower and even more so, because there is less of an angle to the pharynx. When a Eustachian tube runs more horizontally, it tends to become blocked or filled with fluid. This has a tendency to lead to the development of otitis media, or more simply, ear infection.

When Lisa was a couple of months old, I thought she was fussier than normal. My first thought, of course, was her heart because that was the main concern from her pediatrician, which in turn led us to take Lisa to her first visit with a cardiology specialist. Now, with this new fussiness, she would become a little dusky colored when she cried, and it made me think she was developing some more problems with her heart. She wasn't eating well or sleeping as soundly, which was unusual for her. I was unsure of my skills as a mother and caretaker, even after tending to my three other children who were born before Lisa. I wanted to take her to the doctor. The only trouble was the timing. It was a weekend and it was evening, and the doctor's office was closed. As my husband and I were driving her to the hospital, I rationalized that the emergency room visit would be the best place if indeed it was her heart. Now, I just had to explain THAT to the emergency room physician. After our arrival, all the regular exam procedures were done, including taking her temperature, checking her pulse, and looking into her nose and ears. The doctor listened to her heart several times and then looked at us with a serious-looking, somber face. Oh no, I thought, here it comes. It's her heart. Well, it turned out to be something else. He diagnosed ear infection. He also said her heart sounds were interesting, which kept him listening a little longer, but according to him, things sounded stable.

But wait, he's telling us she had EAR infection! I never thought that might be the problem. We left there with a bunch of sample products, which always helped with our finances. I felt a little foolish, but a lot relieved. And that was my first lesson with Lisa. Always expect ear infection before anything else and rightly so, because she had it a lot; at least monthly, if not more often. She had ear infection when she had a cold or congestion, when she was cutting teeth, and even when she seemed to be fine. She was always on medication.

I remember taking her to a well-baby checkup, and being told she had ear infection. She wasn't fussy at all, but had cut down on her eating. Lesson number two: if she doesn't eat as much as usual, she has ear infection. I guessed her pain tolerance was so high that she no longer noticed or felt the discomfort and that her crying wouldn't help to make it better. And then again, maybe it just hurt more when she cried. Whatever it was, I had to really be aware of her total disposition, to always watch for ear infections. I checked her ears constantly, looking for any drainage. Usually by that time, if it was draining it meant her eardrum had ruptured, and that would mean the inner pressure and pain was actually relieved. But too many ruptured eardrums were not good either, so catching her ear infection early was important. As it was, she had tubes in both of her ears, four times.

There was a time when she had such bad congestion during the winter that I thought it felt like spring would never arrive. And through it all, she maintained her regular bouts of ear infections. But, worse than that, was the croup she got. She had this weird resonant barking cough, and seemed to have more trouble than usual with her breathing. First, we tried a humidifier in her room, but that just didn't help much. Finally, the doctor told us to wrap her up warmly and take her outside. The air was cold, and this seemed to help some. We still couldn't completely clear it up, which resulted in her ending up in the hospital for several days, under a clear plastic tent that held the cool, moist air in for her to breath. She was also given breathing treatments with some medicine. She had to wear a facemask, which she didn't like. We had to hold the mask on, and at the same time try keep her hands off of it. Five minutes can be a long time when you have to keep her preoccupied. But the medicine helped, and within a couple of days, she was able to go home.

Lisa usually took medicine pretty well, but there were times when she was rather impossible with the whole concept of medicine taking. Taking medicine by mouth was fairly easy when it was a liquid. Keeping it in her mouth when she was a baby was a little more difficult though. When we used a regular kitchen teaspoon, I knew I wasn't getting an exact dose as it spilled all over her face most of the time. At that point, I didn't know whether to give her a little more or just wait until the next dose. It was really great when I found the handy medicine spoons that allowed me to pour the medicine into the handle. It had measurement lines on the side, so you knew just exactly how much medicine was being given. The only problem left to solve was the medicine that ran out of her mouth. With "the spoon," it was easier to control because it would be poured slower. You could also scoop any medicine that ran out of the sides of her mouth with the spoon. This way you could save most of it and try to pour it back in the mouth. That spoon was the best invention ever. I bought several, and in case one broke or I lost one or left home without one, I'd always have a spare. They also came in different colors, which was nice when we had more than one child on medicine. They each had their own color. The only time we had trouble after "the spoon" was if the medicine tasted awful. And in that case, we just did the best we could and got it down fast.

We did learn that if the child would not swallow what was in the mouth, you could pinch their nostrils closed, which made them want to take a breath. This would be more like a gulp, and the liquid medicine would go down. We had to be careful because they could also gag or cough, and that liquid could end up all over the front of the child and you.

As Lisa grew, we gradually switched her over to tablet form. She was able to take those pretty good, probably because she got a lot of practice taking the tablet form of medicine. Sometimes we would have to put it in some applesauce or other food substance, to get her to swallow it, but once she learned how to take tablets, it wasn't a big deal. One trick was to make sure she had it towards the back of her mouth before she swallowed it. Otherwise, she would just have it floating around her mouth, dissolving and tasting really bad. Another thing to remember was to not tip her backwards; not even to have her tip her head back. That actually closes off or changes the passageway of the pharynx, and makes it more difficult to swallow. As an adult, I can and do put my chin down slightly, which makes swallowing easier. Trying to get a child to do this is somewhat more difficult. It was fairly easy to switch Lisa over to tablet form and such a blessing when we would travel. No liquid to pack or spill, no refrigeration needed. There were times, before tablet medicine, when I would bring a small 6-pack cooler to store liquid antibiotics when we took a road trip. Not anymore. I thought we'd never get past the need for medicine, but there was a light at the end of that tunnel. There was a time when Lisa had taken so many different antibiotics that she'd run out of choices, because their effectiveness was diminished due to the continuous use. That is no longer true. Isolated incidents can now be resolved with a regular 10-day supply of an antibiotic. She still does take medicine occasionally, but it's not near the volume as when she was little. Another happy ending. She survived and so did our checkbook.

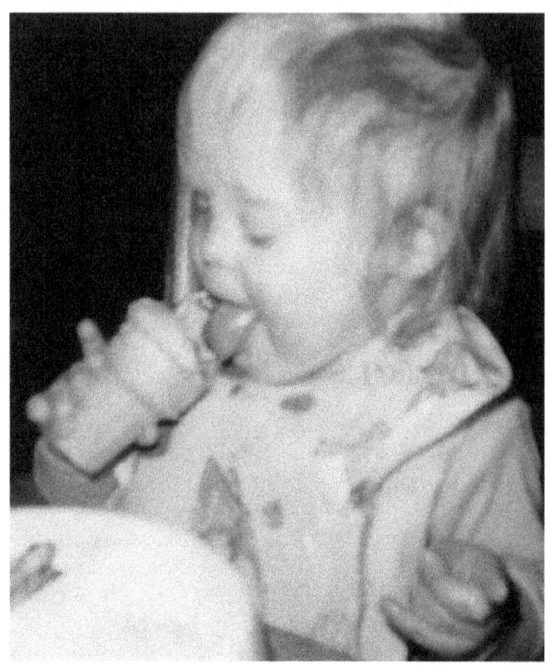

Ear Infections Plentiful

For our family, any month in the year was a good time to have an ear infection. In the winter months, I thought a stocking cap and scarf could make a difference, but the ear infections occurred just the same. In the summer months, swimming seemed to be a problem because water would get in their ears and not know how to get out. Spring and fall must have had some connection with allergies and sinus problems, because several of my kids had runny noses, coughs and sneezes, which always turned into an ear infection. And I'm not talking about just Lisa when it comes to ear infection at our house. Her older brother also tried to put us in the poor house with his chronic ear problems.

I could always tell when he had ear infection because he would change from busy and talkative to quiet and docile. The quiet was nice, but not at the expense of him being ill. With Lisa, I think she started her life with an ear infection. At two or three months old, we had to take her to the emergency room, where she and I both cried. She bawled due to the discomfort of bulging eardrums, and I from worry about how she could possibly be so miserable. I didn't think of ear infection at that young age; maybe because in remembering her birth, the diagnosis was major heart troubles. Whew, it wasn't her heart this time. Did I say "Yea, it's just an ear infection!?!"

As it turned out, Lisa was the winner with the most ear infections in any given month. She also had those cute little tubes put in her ears more than her brothers and sister. On four different occasions, they were inserted to allow for better drainage and to lessen the occurrence of infection. I was never quite sure about their effect. The first two sets of tubes fell out almost immediately, the third set took a little longer to leave and the last set must have been "just right," because she did not need another set.

During one of my late night sessions of giving medicine and TLC (tender loving care) to those who were suffering from ear infection at my house, I envisioned an elite organization for parents. It was a club with no officers, because we would all be busy juggling medicine schedules. The meetings would be held in the Doctor's waiting area, because we spent a lot of time there. Decisions made at this time would be with the majority in agreement, but please don't ask the sleeping parent to vote on anything. Just let them sleep until someone calls their child's name; then wake them so they can get into the exam room for the doctor to see the sick child. The dues would be your doctor bill and prescription. Note, if this charge exceeds $5, which it usually does when the liquid gold medicine is ordered, you are automatically exempt from club dues. If you qualify for this organization, please don't call me, call your doctor.

Ear infections unanimously! That's right, I said unanimously. We parents are all in this together. We have a name; we share the same views, the same problems, so let's start a club. Need to join the club? I'm sure no one *wants* to join, but if you meet the following requirements, you are in, no charge, except of course when you have to pay the bill from the doctor.

Qualifications

1. Have you taken your child in for a well-baby checkup, only to discover an ear infection?

2. Have you taken your child in for any illness, from a cold to a knee scrape, only to discover an ear infection?

3. Have you taken your child in for what you are sure is ear infection, only to discover anything but ear infection?

4. Do you pay the doctor by the visit (every ten days), by the month, or $10 a payday for life?

5. From birth to age one, or until after having tubes inserted, is your sleep schedule disrupted nightly by "ouchy" ears?

6. Do you see an ear specialist on a regular basis; know him by his first name, plus his wife's, children's and pet's name?

7. Do you know three different numbers to call to get in to see one doctor or another?

8. Is your child's baby book filled with little armbands from the numerous hospital visits to have ventilation or ear tubes put in?

9. Is your kitchen windowsill, medicine chest or special safe filled with an assortment of eardrops, sulphur medicine, non-aspirin and thermometers?

10. If you have more than one child who qualifies, do you have a sheet taped to the refrigerator stating times for medicine, to whom, what kind and for how many days?

11. Does your insurance have a deductible that you meet in February or March of every year?

12. Is summer time just as bad as any other time for those never-ending ear problems?

13. Do you keep repeating those famous words "They will outgrow it." Let's hope they do. And, we want to welcome you to the club!

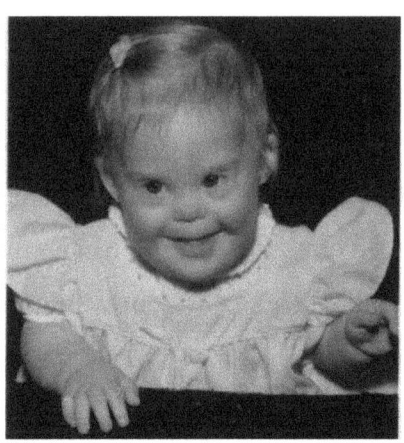

Losing the First Tooth

When that first tooth comes in, parents always make a big fuss. It was as if the child had to work really hard to get that tooth through their gum line, when all they really had to do was wait and let nature do the rest.

Some kids spend many long nights, never days, fussing, crying and drooling just to cut their first tooth. Other times, the tooth just shows up without warning or fanfare, usually when you least expect it. I remember hearing a slight "click" noise with each bite while feeding a child with a long-handled baby spoon. And when I looked in the child's mouth, there it was; a teeny-tiny, sharp white tooth, which poked through the tender red gum line on the bottom. Of course, this wasn't one of my kids. It only happened when I fed my sisters' children. My kids fed themselves long before they ever had a tooth and with Lisa, that was a LONG time.

Lisa was not your ordinary, run of the mill, textbook follower when it comes to teeth, but then none of my kids followed the book on this topic. They were all at least a year old before experiencing the pain of that first tooth, and I don't think they were too fussy either. I really don't remember a lot of fussy nights, but as I get older, I think the memories of those sleepless nights just slowly fade away.

I do know Lisa started drooling long before we ever thought of her having a tooth, but I'm sure her mouth, facial structure and large tongue contributed to her drooling. We worked a lot on getting her to close her mouth, keep her tongue in and to swallow, which helped decrease the drooling. In the broad scheme of things, I think this must have helped her decreased drooling. She also chewed on lots of things, but I think it was because we taught her to do this. I still can't believe that we did that, but it's true! And, you must remember that one of her goals from her homebound teacher was to help her explore items by allowing her to use her mouth. We spent a lot of time placing objects in her hand, and bringing them to her mouth so she could chew or goober all over the object. Of course, a later goal for her was to keep inappropriate objects out of her mouth. How contradictory! But, I can say she learned that goal exceptionally well.

Lisa's first tooth came in on top, but not a front tooth like most kids. When she smiled, there was that one tiny, shiny canine tooth and no front teeth. She looked so funny, but cute. She was also over a year old at the time, had been gumming all her food for quite awhile and yet had no problems eating the same table foods we ate.

I think her gums must have been the strongest ever. Maybe that's why she had such a time with losing her teeth. Her gums just wouldn't let go! At the age of 7½, she finally got a loose tooth. When I first discovered it was loose, I got really excited, knowing we would soon experience another "first" with her. Weeks later, the excitement dwindled. I got tired of seeing the tooth off center and half out, but still hanging onto the gum line in her mouth.

I think her older siblings were also tired of it. They would talk to Lisa till they were blue in the face, trying to convince her to pull it out. They even tried to bribe her with her favorite candy and "two Band-Aids." (She had a thing for Band-Aids, and would do anything to get one as a reward.) Can you believe she turned all that down, just to keep that loose, wobbly tooth in her mouth? Her brothers and sister spent over an hour one evening making promises galore, and giving Lisa lots of attention. Conversation centered on who would be the next that Lisa would choose to let them "wiggle" her tooth. Some of those wiggles seemed pretty rough. They tried to tie dental floss around the loose tooth, but Lisa wouldn't keep her mouth open long enough and the floss kept slipping off. They also tried to grab hold of the tooth using a tissue, so their fingers wouldn't slip. Nothing seemed to work to release that tooth from the strong gum line.

All they accomplished with their efforts was to have an upset little girl who mistakenly ate some of the tissue. I had my camera ready to snap the exciting event when it happened, but all I got were a couple of pictures of my four kids in the bathroom, peering at the mirror with their mouths open. They were trying to show Lisa what to do. It didn't work, but it sure produced a candid, funny picture.

One evening after lots of encouragement with no results, it was bedtime for Lisa. The other kids moaned and groaned for "just one more minute." No use; the tooth was still there, loose and off centered. She went to bed and slept soundly. When I got Lisa up for school the next morning, her hand immediately went to her mouth and she felt her loose tooth. She exclaimed "It's still in there!" She seemed relieved. Maybe it's tough to part with something you've had for so long.

She finally did get it out, when it was just hanging by a thread. That seemed to excite her, because she knew the tooth would be placed in a glass of water and left for the tooth fairy. The tooth fairy made a visit that night, deposited some money, and took the tooth away. This ritual was the same as with all our kids, with only one exception. That tooth fairy filed the tooth in Lisa's baby book. After all that hard work, don't you think it should be saved?

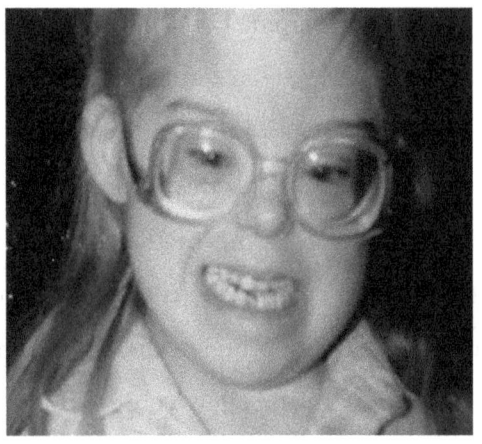

Lisa the 'Unsinkable'

As an infant, Lisa's only contact with water was during bath time. She was not given a chance to splash in a baby pool or go to the city pool to swim very often. Her younger years were spent in and out of doctor's offices and she had many ear infections and surgeries. I insisted she not have swim lessons, especially if that would increase her chances for recurrent ear infections. Though not the latest fashion rage, Lisa did wear some of those specially molded earplugs when in the water, which helped prevent some of those nasty recurrent infections. It was quite a few years before she no longer had tubes in her ears or needed those special plugs. I finally agreed for her to try swim lessons and was surprised by her excitement after all those years of being kept from the water.

She was hesitant but not really afraid of the water when she was little. She just seemed to develop a stronger fear as she got older. Tub time was always fun, and I remember a few incidents when she slipped and slid back and forth in the tub, ending up under water. I didn't think that traumatized her. She never refused a bath. She also enjoyed the six-foot (in diameter) plastic kiddie wading pool we had set up in our back yard throughout the hot summer months. She really thought she was swimming, when all she did was a belly crawl back and forth and 'round and 'round. I thought she'd wear off the cute ducky pictures on the floor of the pool. Sometimes she'd kick her feet or try to splash her hands in the six inches of water. She took care to not get her face or head wet. If she ended up slipping and going under, she would come up coughing and sputtering, and being very vocal about the incident.

We didn't make swimming a priority; partly because of all the ear infections she had for many years, summer and winter. We really started to encourage her to participate more when we signed her up for swim lessons. Thank goodness there were some very patient swim instructors. During the first "real" set of lessons, Lisa spent most of her "water time" in the arms of the instructor. Once or twice a swim instructor, while in the water, would hold her on her stomach and she was encouraged to kick. No problem there. She kicked a lot, trying to get out of this position and back in someone's arms. They tried to encourage her to put her face in the water, but not much happened with that activity either. She just didn't want to be under water, I guess.

On her first day of the session, Lisa was ready hours ahead of schedule. She got up that morning with the words "swim lessons" on her lips, and I heard about it all day. She dressed in her one piece, multicolored suit, grabbed a big beach towel, goggles and her sandals and announced she was ready. I had to explain to her about time, about waiting and about the need to have a few clothes on because there was snow outside. Her lessons were held at an indoor pool.

When lesson time finally arrived, we took off for the pool. On the way, she related all she knew about swimming, which sounded like a lot. She talked about holding her breath, turning her head side to side to breath, and wanting to be a fast swimmer like her brother. When we arrived at the pool, something happened to change her mind. She went into the pool area, but would not walk down the steps into the shallow end of the pool. She only agreed to sit on the ledge of the pool and dangle her feet in the water. She would also lie on her tummy, with her knees bent and feet swinging in the air while she splashed the water with her hands. But she would not get in the pool.

It took eight weeks of reassurance, along with a patient teacher, to get her moving while *in* the water. Once in, she picked up some very helpful hints. Hint number one, you need to blow bubbles when your face is in the water, or you may end up having to gargle with the water instead. Hint number two, do not drink the water, which she did a lot. Hint number three, stay in the shallow water. Lisa found out if she walked out where the water went past her upper chest or shoulders, her feet lifted off the bottom of the pool and she was no longer able to touch it. That was big trouble!

Her first eight-week session ended with notations about her progress, suggestions and no certificate. It was recommended she repeat this beginner class at least once more. I knew that would be the case. She needed *lots* of sessions. As it turned out, she ended up not swimming again for about a year. Yup, more ear infections.

When we finally discussed swim lessons again, Lisa was ready, willing and able. She was excited about getting back in the water, and once again I heard about swimming from morning until the actual time arrived. She had matured in her tactics, and would say things like "I know swimming is at 5 o'clock. Just how many hours until then?" or "I'll get dressed in my suit now, and not say any more about it until 5 o'clock."

Lisa was definitely excited. Best of all, she had no problem getting in the water. Once ready, she walked out of the locker area and headed to the pool. She walked around in the water, jumped up and down and happily splashed herself. She took to the instructor immediately, and tried everything that was asked of her.

Our amazing Lisa mastered blowing bubbles and put her entire face in the water on her first day. Through the next several weeks, she used a kickboard to float across the width of the pool, and allowed someone to hold her flat on her stomach in the water, with her arms stretched out and no kickboard. She was even willing to attempt the back float, after lots of encouragement and reassurance. But if you tried to let go of her in this position, watch out. She would grab wildly at anything that was near her and yell loudly "Ah, ah, ah" several times. She was never in deep water so the instructor would calmly tell her to put her feet down to touch the bottom.

Slowly, her confidence worked into unflinching boldness. At one session, she put her face in the water, and almost covered her entire head. When she came up for a breath, she grabbed the side of the wall, made a thumbs-up sign to the instructor and hollered "Unsinkable!"

This was short lived, for as she turned to walk away after her triumph, she lost her footing, slipped and went all the way under water. This time she came out coughing water, with a look of surprise that said, "How could this have happened to the unsinkable?" During another episode an instructor was helping her with rotary, or side-to-side breathing. They didn't try to arm movements though, as that was too confusing for Lisa.

As it happened, Lisa put her face in the water, turned to the side, then quickly back in the water, continuing this pattern with her mouth continually tightly closed. Her eyes were closed, her head became shaky, and her cheeks distended from holding her breath, definitely ready to burst. Her instructor kept telling her to "Breathe, breathe." Soon she stopped, let out all her air in a big huff, and said breathlessly, "I am, I am." So much for breathing.

It took her quite awhile to master the art of swimming, but in time she did. From her early years until she was in seventh grade, Lisa had lots of lessons. She was a trooper, trying everything that she was told to do and never gave up. The surprise was she finally just took off and started swimming on her own. But, that's a different story.

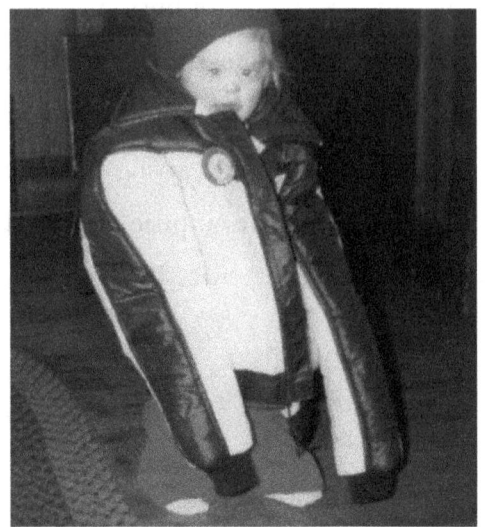

Shopping for Clothes

Finding clothes for Lisa has never been easy. I was never able to go by sizes in relationship to her age, because everything was always too long. If the length fit, it was usually too tight around the waist. We improvised with the hand me downs, because I didn't feel too bad about cutting the pant legs shorter after her sister and two older cousins had worn them. But to cut something new was almost unbearable for me. Once in awhile, I could find some short-legged elastic-waist pants that fit fairly well. If the waist were ever too large, I would take it in on the sides, to make it close fitting. This was very important when she was learning to walk. Her pants always seem to fall down, mostly because she had no hips to hold her pants up.

We tried using a belt, but her paunchy stomach would be rubbed or bothered by the confinement and she'd want it off. If the belt came off by her own doing, then usually the pants also came off, either because they were so loose that they fell off or she pulled them off. We tried suspenders, but this wasn't much better. A lot of times they'd be pulled up really tight, and instead of staying gripped to the pants, one strap would pull away and cause a major obstacle when she walked. If they happened to stay attached to the pants, they would invariably slip off her shoulders. There's a knack to keeping straps up, and she didn't have it. I sewed some small, one-fourth inch wide strips to the tops of the shirts that didn't have straps, just to hold the suspenders in place. This helped the suspenders situation a little.

Making sure the pants stayed up was real important, especially after she started walking. She didn't need any more obstacles to hinder her progress. We also had to roll up the bottom of the pants into cuffs just to keep them out of the way. Usually, we did four or five rolls up from the bottom, only to have so much weight around the ankles that her balance was probably affected.

I tried to buy outfits that had pants and a top as two pieces, but only from your mix and match choices. There were also the nicer, dressier outfit sets but these were not made for crawling, just sitting. She had very few outfits of this kind, because they never fit quite right. With a matched set of clothing, if you got the top to fit, the matching pants were way too big. If the pants fit, the shirt was tight. If we got real lucky and the shirt was looser, with the pants still fitting, the shirtsleeves would be too long. She had, actually still has, lots of rolled up sleeves, which goes well with the rolled up pants. Nothing ever fit quite right. Her size and shape just didn't fit into the normal clothes. When we chose clothing, I looked for the easiest fasteners available. Snaps and zippers were easier than hooks and buttons, but even snaps had to be checked out for ease in fastening. Some snaps are big, bulky and difficult to snap. The real trick after that was pulling them apart again. That takes a lot of muscle and finger dexterity, which Lisa didn't have when she was younger. It was good practice to use snaps occasionally, but it was also easier to practice with a piece of clothing on the table instead of something she was wearing. Zippers were another option, but the problem with that was in getting the zipper aligned just right to get it started.

Sliding one side into another before the actual zipping took lots of practice. At first we started all her zippers then let her finish the zipping up part. It was actually a long time before she could do it all by herself. It was also easier to zip while not wearing the object, so Lisa practiced this a lot at the table. I remember how Lisa put on her coat before she mastered zipping up a coat while wearing it. She would lay the coat on the table or floor, upside down, with the arm sleeves pointing out and up. After that, Lisa would put her arms in the sleeves, and the coat out in front of her. At this point, she would swing her arms up over her head and down, bringing the coat behind her, and she'd have it on correctly. This worked real slick, but it left her coat unzipped. After she learned to zip, she tried to zip it up ahead of time, and try this new dressing technique, but oops, it just didn't work. She'd slip her arms in, then her head, and there the coat would stay, zipper in the back, with her neck collar around her knees. It's difficult to walk that way.

Walking was bad enough for her, but sometimes it was made more difficult because of her shoes. We had a terrible time finding her size in shoes. Her feet were short and narrow, and her heels were so tiny that almost everything slipped off, even when we had them tied tight with a double knot. We tried heel inserts, but they weren't easily transferred to other pairs of shoes. The adhesive didn't stick after a couple of times, either. Tying the laces took some time, and that time increased when Lisa was learning to tie her own shoes. That skill took a long time for her to master, and was sabotaged with the invention of Velcro. I thought this would eliminate the need for her to ever tie her shoes. However, I also tried to think ahead, and realized that not every pair of shoes she would ever own would be with Velcro instead of laces. I decided that learning to tie shoes would still be a good skill to have.

Teaching her to tie shoes was fun and frustrating. We even had the teachers at school helping her. But, at some point we realized that two different techniques were being used, and it's no wonder we were confusing her. Using the shoelaces, the two "rabbit ears" was not the same as taking the "bunny around the tree trunk and push it through the other side" technique. Once we were all on the same page, she mastered tying shoes. They were never tight enough, so she had to keep re-tying them a lot. We finally taught her to do a double knot, which helped keep the laces together even better. Now she mastered this skill, but I still felt Velcro was a good invention.

Some shirts were easier for her with the Velcro fasteners, but for pants they were bad news. Her paunchy stomach kept popping the Velcro loose. A buttonhole in the pants was also difficult to master. Consequently, snaps were the best choice for Lisa. As she's grown up, she has had a better selection of clothes and an easier time with the fasteners. Shopping for clothes for Lisa is still a challenge. I know there are some places where adaptive clothing can be obtained for those with dressing difficulties. This is a great idea, but I think we've done pretty good adapting her clothing as her needs and challenges arose.

Learning to Swim

Lisa has never been very athletic or competitive in sports. Her physical abilities were directly related to her desire and need. She did learn to ride a big wheel and a tricycle, but so far not a bike without the training wheels. She did like playing on the park toys: merry go 'round, teeter-totter and swings. These were things that didn't require her to move a lot. She was just as happy sitting and watching others play most of the time. Swimming was one sport I thought she'd never master, just because it was clearly not a favorite sport for her. During her younger years, the regular swim lessons just didn't seem to do a lot for her. We switched her to swimming with the Special Olympics group because a volunteer specifically said she would help Lisa, teaching her to swim and help her to feel more comfortable in the water. I went and watched their technique, thinking they would really do something great for her and her swimming. I have to give them credit for trying, but it was not meant to be. The Special Olympics volunteer began with letting Lisa sit on the steps that went down into the water. This was just to get her acclimated to the water. "You know, water is our friend." This tactic could have been a mistake, because Lisa wouldn't leave her safe spot on the top step when they wanted her to be on top of the water, to kick, splash or try to go under. She just sat on those steps that descended into the water, never actually getting off them to get lower into the water.

The instructors finally convinced her that if she got off the steps, she could stand right next to the steps, and just swim towards them. Within a space of three feet, she would face the steps, stretch out her arms and then try to float forward to the steps. Her feet never left the pool floor, and her head never touched the water. She literally walked to the steps, with her arms stretched out in front of her, where she'd sit until someone told her to do it again. Then she would walk down and off the steps, turn around and "swim" back again. Frankly, I didn't think that should count as swimming.

Finally, she wasn't allowed to be by the steps, but could remain in the shallow end. This wasn't good, because even with standing in the shallow, Lisa was almost under water. She was, and still is really short. The water level came to her upper chest near the armpit area, and she had a difficult time keeping her feet grounded. Because of this, she bobbed a lot; but not without support from the side of the pool. She hung on to the side most of the time, only letting go to pass another swimmer who also laid claim to the wall. She did get away from the side occasionally, but she was never able to really feel comfortable in a very large pool, and definitely not ready for Special Olympic competition. That all changed when we moved to a newer house in another state.

By some bit of luck or coincidence, the house we liked and eventually bought just happened to have an in-ground pool. Lisa wasn't too thrilled one way or another, but one of her brothers was a swimmer from way back in grade school, and was thrilled to know that he could now have his own private practice pool. He also gave private lessons, which was the beginning of Lisa's swimming. In the summer months he would teach one or two students at a time throughout the week, and Lisa would sit inside, watching through the sliding glass doors that opened up the to poolside area. At first, she just watched. When we would swim later in the day as a family, she would wear her arm or back floats, use a kick board or other float device and stay in the shallow end near the steps.

Because we had daily access to a pool, or because it was only family, we started to notice a difference in Lisa and her water skills. I would actually call it swimming, because that's what she was doing by the end of the summer. The interesting thing was the variety of skills she exhibited. It seemed like overnight Lisa could float without help, arms and legs fully extended. She could put her face in the water, kick and actual propel forward. She still had her floats on, but she ventured into the deep without assistance, swimming end to end, going the length of the pool. She had a nice, smooth stroke, her hands and arms nicely slicing the surface water with very little splash. She did not slap, splash or flail them noisily or wildly. Consequently, she moved effectively and quickly, actually gaining yardage with each move. It took her awhile to learn rotary breathing, but she kept her face down in the water while swimming, not up above the water like she used to do.

Her lung capacity was challenged during this time, especially when she swam the width of a regulation size pool. When she started to swim a lap across the pool, she did not take a breath, because this slowed her down. In order for her to take a breath during Special Olympics competitions, Lisa would stop her stroke, assume an upright position in the water, kicking her legs to keep her afloat, take a breath and quickly go back to her stroke. At some point, she must have figured it was easier to just hold her breath as long as possible and just swim. She did amazingly well, nearly making it the entire width by just holding her breath. She won a few ribbons and medals, but to me, she won a lot more. She learned how to not be afraid of the water, and in the process, learned how to swim. She also learned how to work at something in her own way, by observing and after that trying it, in order to be a success.

Down Syndrome: Making a Difference in Others

When Lisa was younger, I would introduce her to others and not say anything about her having Down syndrome. It was obvious to me that she had Down syndrome, and if other people had questions, I would answer them truthfully. I felt I could explain her small size and shortcomings without stating her disability. In doing so, I believed I was protecting her and myself. That theory really didn't work well. Lisa has Down syndrome, and that couldn't be changed. I soon decided that what I could do is educate others on the facts and show the unlimited potential for people with Down syndrome.

One time while on vacation, we stayed at a motel with an indoor pool. Isn't this a prerequisite when choosing a motel? Lisa wanted to go swimming, so I helped her get ready. She had two white floats, one strapped to her chest and the other on her back. She also wanted to have those plastic blow-up floaties that could be moved to the upper arms. As we were walking out the door to go down to the pool, Lisa remembered the circular ring that could be slipped over her head and be worn around her waist. Now, she was ready to swim.

We got to the pool's edge and Lisa couldn't figure out how she was going to get in the water with all the paraphernalia on. She was too scared to walk down the steps, because she did not have her glasses on and it was difficult for her to look down because of her depth perception issues. She could not sit on the side of the pool and slip in feet first, because the floats got caught on the edge. I finally told her I would help, and that seemed to make things better for her. After I got Lisa into the water, I walked around in the pool with her, but encouraged her to do some paddling and practice staying afloat. That wasn't so difficult with all those floats on. There was no way she would sink, but I couldn't convince her of that. She stayed close to the pool edge, and did very little floating.

Soon, two young girls were in the pool and somewhat curious about Lisa. They kept looking at her, then talking to themselves in whispers. I wanted to say something, but I really didn't know what they were thinking or discussing.

Were they upset because someone like Lisa, someone with Down syndrome, was in the pool with them? Or were they curious because she had all those floats on? I felt very conspicuous, so I got busy and took Lisa towards the deeper water.

As we neared the dividing rope, she yelled for me not to let her go, and to hurry and get her over to the edge of the pool. She was somewhat loud and her voice echoed in the closed-in pool area. Once again she generated attention from those two girls. They came closer to Lisa and watched her. I said "Hi" and asked where they were from. I figured my small talk could make them forget about Lisa's noisy episode. The girls were friendly enough and willing to visit. They also had questions about Lisa, like why was she so scared of the water, why did she have those floats on and how old was she?

I tried to explain that Lisa had not spent much time in the water because of ear infections and the reason for the floats was to give her some security. Lisa answered that she was nine, and this surprised the girls. They could see that Lisa was definitely smaller than either one of them, and she could not swim, even though they could at their young age of seven.

They questioned Lisa's age, and asked me if she was really nine. I tried to explain her size to them, without bringing up the fact that she had Down syndrome. I just didn't think it was necessary to mention that yet.

I brought Lisa back to the shallow end of the pool and let go of her. As I walked away from her and the girls, they continued to talk and play together. I felt good about this interaction, yet felt a little uneasy that I did not tell them about the Down syndrome.

Soon, one girl asked me if Lisa had Down syndrome like that boy on television…"You know the one, Corky, on Life Goes On." [9] Their casual comment let me know this fact didn't bother them, so I said yes she does, and began to explain Down syndrome. They weren't interested. They just wanted to play with Lisa. The girls were curious about Lisa's floats and her age, not her syndrome. To those girls, Lisa was just another new friend.

It wasn't necessary for those girls to have the textbook facts on Lisa, but I know many people who do need to know about Down syndrome before they can see past that to discover a lovely, young lady like Lisa.

I have since learned to be more open with others, knowing I can't protect Lisa from the general public or the public from Lisa. But, by helping Lisa to do her best, and by talking to others, I can make a difference in the way people think, react and accept Lisa and hopefully, for all those who have Down syndrome.

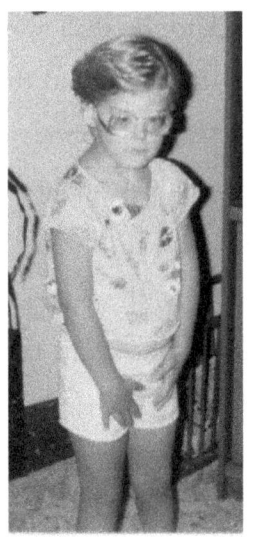

First Haircut

Lisa had her first word, her first step, a first loose tooth, followed by a first haircut. Now mind you, she had her bangs and her long, blond, waist-length hair trimmed, sometimes as much as 3-4 inches, but CUT, no, this was definitely not a word associated with Lisa's hair for many years. At some point, and for many months, she had been begging me to go to the "booty" shop, (that's beauty in English). Many times I'd take her with one of her brothers, to watch them while they got their hair cut, but she grew more insistent with each visit to have her own hair cut. I became a little concerned though, when her haircut request was a butch or all shaved, like her brothers.

I finally agreed to have it cut, so we looked around at different styles. I needed something easy, manageable and simple for me to style. I had one other requirement; I did not want her to have a cut that would draw attention to her or her disability. I was specifically thinking of those long ago bowl cuts that I seemed to think was the look of an institutionalized resident at a state facility.

The beautician went right to work, getting Lisa situated in the big chair that had a booster chair inserted for her. First obstacle, getting the hair washed. Lisa had to be leaned back, which seemed to scare her to death. Her piercing scream had everyone looking on. I was ready to pick her up, wrap a towel around her wet head and take her home. We made it through the hair washing after a lot of promises, bribes and encouragement. Now it was time for me to scream. The beautician pulled out a sharp, shiny pair of scissors, pulled the hair together at the nape, and said "We'll just cut this off here so it's easier to work with." Snip. Too late now! Just as quickly as she said this, the hair fell to the floor and scattered all over. Lisa had a hard time keeping her hands under the big plastic apron that she had on. She constantly reached back and fluffed the short bob, which got shorter with each snip. I must admit, the end result was cute, even though I believed it kind of looked like someone put a bowl on her head. Just what I thought I didn't want.

Now I started spending my mornings curling her hair, not braiding it, as I did with her long hair before it was cut. My main task was to reassure her that I would not touch *her* with the hot iron, just her hair. It took a lot of talking. I must also admit, the new style changed Lisa. She could now wash and comb it herself, which gave her a sense of self-confidence and self-esteem. She took pride in how she looked and she felt good about herself. You could see this when you watched her primping in front of the bathroom mirror. She would hold the brush just right, and slowly comb it just the way she wanted, with a big smile on her face during this enjoyable chore. It was a real ego booster for her.

For me, it meant she was growing up a little more. She was able to choose to have her haircut, and now depended less on me to care for her. This was sad for me, but very important for her and her future. Isn't it strange how important a hair cut can be?

A Short Haircut

When Lisa was a baby, she didn't have a whole lot of hair, and what she did have was very fine and silky. This hair of hers was also stubborn. There were not a whole lot of products that would keep the hair in place or keep it from being full of static. I'm not sure what came first, her hair or her personal nature, but they both ended up being stubborn.

As her hair grew, I learned how to put in those plastic barrettes of varying sizes, shapes and colors. This was not easy, because of her tender scalp and fine hair. If I used one end of the barrette to gather up the hair or to make a part, I had to be careful not to poke her or drag it along the surface of the scalp. She squirmed a bit with any hair activity at first, but the barrettes were the worst. As her hair grew, I tried different styles and tactics to get that style just right. One mistake I made was to give her bangs in the very beginning. Later on, I wanted them to grow long, thinking no bangs would be easier. Maybe so, but the waiting period was awful. The barrettes came in handy at that time, but she looked funny with them clipped in front, making her hair look like drapes drawn off to either side of her forehead by those plastic barrettes.

Lisa's two older brothers got haircuts quite regularly, but she only got a trim occasionally. When she realized this and knew what a Mohawk cut was, that was all she talked about. Now, her brothers had never had a Mohawk, but they did have some unusual styles on occasion. I don't know why she wanted the Mohawk style, but every time I would trim her hair, she would give that request. One of her brothers must have wanted to help, because he was a key participant in one of Lisa's unusual cuts. Her hair was long, at least past her shoulders in length. At that time she had bangs, and I had pulled her hair back on the sides, off her face and used rubber bands to hold those sections of hair in place on either side of her head, just above the ears. I left the rest of her hair down in the back, so it was not all taken up into the sides that I had secured with the rubber bands. I can't imagine that her brother had more than a moment to take a "professional" look at her hair, and thank goodness his barber skills were short lived. As it was, when I walked in the room, there he was, with the scissors in one hand and one of the side ponytails in the other, not attached to the scalp. One fistful of hair, gone. There was not much to work with on that side to cover the empty section but I did come up with a reasonable solution. I parted her hair on the opposite side, and let the hair fall over the bare spot. This actually didn't look too bad. I was really glad I hadn't put it in full pigtails or a ponytail. It ended up being a much smaller portion than what could have happened. It took months of growing and trimming before it really looked good again.

    Lisa had her hand at using the scissors several times, too, but she did the very common cut done by all kids. (at least all mine did). This was the famous "above one eyebrow bangs cut." Of course, way too much was whacked off, so there was no way to trim the other side to match or to cover up the empty spot with hair from another part of her scalp, like those all too familiar comb overs. We had to suffer through the growing out period with stares and laughter from others. The sad thing was, she did it more than once, and usually right before school pictures. But even so, those are memories worth saving, too; don't you agree with me about that?

The first time she snipped her bangs, I tried to give some positive focus to this dilemma. She did this on her own. Doesn't that mean she can use her cognitive skills to think things through? Wasn't she able to manipulate and use the scissors correctly? She didn't poke an eye out; now that's a big plus. The second time this happened, I wasn't quite so easy going. And that must have been the right approach, because it didn't happen again.

When she wanted her hair cut short, I had a real problem with this. I did not want it short, because again, as with her first haircut, it reminded me of pictures I'd see of people in institutions with the typical "easy, carefree" bowl cut. I didn't want any extra attention drawn to her, so I thought a short cut would not be good. Lisa finally won, and she got a short wedge or layered cut. I had to admit it did look good on her, and it was much easier to manage. At least, I thought so. Again, I used a curling iron to give it some body. Otherwise, it was very straight and lifeless. When Lisa's Dad had to fix her hair, he drew the line at using the curling iron, which was fine with Lisa. She suffered enough burn marks on her ears and neckline from my incompetence in handling the iron. Who knows what may have happened if Dad had to brush *and* use the curling iron. The barrettes were still handy, but not used very often after her hair was cut short. And more than once, after trying to patiently grow her hair long again, Lisa decided she liked it short.

The good thing about a short haircut for Lisa was she could take care of all her hair needs from washing, combing, and even putting on some mousse. We did have to review the art of using mousse; a little is good, a lot is NOT better. What was the first clue? When she could not get her comb through her hair, and to touch her hair felt of hardened gel. I only had to wash the hair twice before the washings brought back its natural light blond color with its fine, flyaway, straight hair. Remember, the key word here is natural.

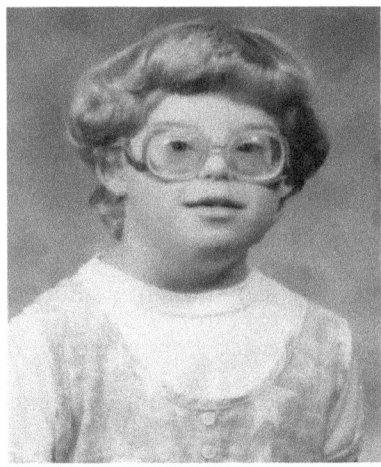

Daycare

Lisa has been in many different types of care programs, from having a babysitter in our own home to going to a babysitter's home, respite care in the home, preschool and regular day care and an after school care program. These are all variations of the same thing, and each was necessary at different stages of her early years. Every time we had to make other arrangements, it felt like we had to take a gamble to try something new. It was out of necessity to make these changes, but it's still a little scary leaving a setting that is familiar and being stretched beyond the comfort zone.

We first opted for a preschool/daycare arrangement when she started attending a school-based early childhood/toddler program in the mornings, at the tender age of three. Up until this time, we hadn't needed daycare, as I was a stay at home mom and all of Lisa's early childhood schooling was done in the home, starting when she was three months old. We began to look for daycare when I started to work outside of the home, and we needed to have someone care for Lisa part of the day. A school van picked her up from our house each morning and transported her to the school-based program. This program released the students before lunch, and instead of bringing her home she went on to her daycare setting. There, lunch was served to her and many other young children who attended this daycare. This was a great place for Lisa to learn other skills, helping out in the kitchen making part of the meal, serving the food and doing cleanup duties. Maybe this was the beginning of her experiences in food service. (She *did* end up with many jobs, in her adult years, at four different food establishments.) Who knew that making peanut butter sandwiches could lead to flipping hamburgers.

This afternoon daycare didn't just do daycare, but they also had a preschool program, and at some point after her early childhood program ended for her, we had her enrolled there as well. A full day of preschool seems like overkill, but she thrived on it. I do believe it contributed to her advancement in perfecting her skills by having continuous schooling. In fact, in the summer, when she only attended the early childhood school-based program, she seemed rather lost at home. Later on, she had school year round and didn't know any different. She easily accepted this, probably because we had started this in her early years and it became the norm for her.

There was a situation when I needed a different daycare setting for a day or so, and I called a place that was recommended and close to where we lived. I began by explaining my situation, and gave some facts about Lisa, her age, past daycare settings and whatever else I could think of that might be important for them to know. As an afterthought, I also said she had Down syndrome. Boy, I thought the phone connection had suddenly been cut off. There was immediate silence at the other end and then just as quickly, the lady started to clear her voice and stammered, asking for me to hold on a minute.

Imagine my surprise when she had the owner get on the phone. Now, the first thing that irritated me was the fact that I had to repeat my situation. I had to describe Lisa and answer what I thought were inappropriate questions. She asked if Lisa was potty trained, and could she walk up and down steps, "because you know this is a two-story building, with lots of steps." She also made references to Lisa having to be well behaved, and able to do things on her own, because they couldn't do everything for her. I had the feeling that mentioning the Down syndrome brought on all these questions, and I was not sure I wanted to go any further in this discussion. But the clincher was when this supposedly educated individual made the comment that I should bring her by so they could SEE her. HUH? This was probably one of the first times I felt my guard go up, my hair stand on end and my claws come out. Part of it was the protective instinct a mother has; part of it was my annoyance of those who don't hear what they are saying or how it comes across. After I gave her my two cents worth, I said thanks, but no thanks. I don't remember what I did for daycare those few days I needed it, but I know I would never take Lisa to that daycare. I also made it a point to discourage others from using that facility. A year later, they had to close down. I'm sure I had nothing to do with that, but I was pleased just the same.

Lisa managed to adjust to different settings and a variety of caregivers, and I feel we were very lucky to have gotten the best of the best. I was even lucky enough to have one neighborhood woman who watched Lisa just one morning a week, while I got out of the house and went bowling. It was a nice break for both Lisa and I. The bonus was, this was the same person who later suggested she have Lisa every morning, for the 20-30 minutes span between when my work time started and when school started for Lisa. Lisa had just started attending the neighborhood school, after years of being bused across town. This was a pilot program, just in the infancy stages. It was new and no one was sure how it would work. By this time, I had acquired a job outside of the home, and my workday started before

Lisa had to be at school. Because of this new wrinkle in our schedule, every morning I'd take her to the neighbor lady and after getting Lisa settled at that house, I would head off to my work place. Lisa would stay at the neighbor's house until school was about to start, and at a designated time, she would walk one short block to school. Bonus! The other great thing about this situation and neighbor was that she lived a lot closer to school than we did. One block instead of four. Consequently, Lisa experienced the joy of walking to school with her classmates.

As far as after school care when she was in the upper elementary grades, she was lucky enough to be at a school that had a program through the local YMCA. This great program, accurately named Almost Home, had been in existence several years. One of Lisa's brothers attended it during the program's first year of operation, and I thought it would be a great place for Lisa, too. When I approached the supervisor in charge, she already knew Lisa, and had no problem enrolling her in the after school care program. I hope that program is still going strong, because it was a great help to our kids and us. Almost Home had some vans that made the rounds to different grade schools, picking up the kids at the end of each day. That transportation was a godsend for parents who worked, and couldn't personally take their children over there when the regular school day was done. On days when there was no school because of a holiday, they had a full, fun day scheduled for the kids at their YMCA based program.

Babysitters and day care was sometimes difficult to find, it was an added expense and sometimes just frustrating. But in all our years of many different settings and caretakers, we have had only the one dreadful incident. Not bad odds!.

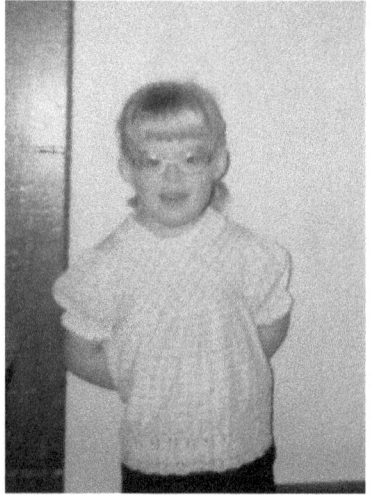

Respite

What is Respite? A reprieve; an interval of rest or relief. But this is easier said than done, especially with four children. Having a child with a disability makes it a little more difficult, because there's always something to be done and it usually takes longer to do certain things. When I heard about a Respite program starting in our town, I wanted to know more.

The program provided respite care to families of children or adults with disabilities. This meant if I wanted to have someone come in on a regular basis to watch Lisa, I could find someone through this program who would help with the care needed for Lisa. Or, for an evening out, arrangements could be made ahead of time, and the Respite provider would watch all the children. It was a welcome and valuable program, but I didn't have the best of luck using it.

Of course, my first concern was the competency of the people who were hired. In researching this program I found out that all the people on the list had been through a certain amount of training, from first aid to basic babysitting. The Program Coordinator arranged for classes and speakers on specific subjects such as Down syndrome, Cerebral Palsy, taking care of someone with tracheotomy, feeding tubes, and a variety of other health related issues. With this selection of classes and speakers, I knew they were well trained. My other problem was I needed someone for *all* of my children, not just for Lisa. Having someone from this program cost a lot more than just hiring the neighborhood teenager, because the program charged by the number of children in the family that needed a babysitter. I remembered some of the regular babysitters in town would charge that way, but I was used to paying someone $1.00 or so an hour, depending on the length of time and what other duties were expected. I am sure we couldn't get by that cheaply in today's babysitting world.

I also know the Respite program had some good training because I sat on a discussion panel that answered their questions about children with disabilities, and to give a parents' point of view on the subject. I also ended up serving on the local board for a while, therefore I felt somewhat obligated to utilize these trained people.

The first one assigned to us was an older person, who only came once. I think having to watch four children was just *too* much for her. She didn't come right out and say that, but I could tell by her nonchalant attitude before hand and her disheveled look afterwards, that she wouldn't be back. She was very polite when she left, saying it was okay, and that yes, she could be called again. Well, I tried once or twice to call for her to come and sit, but soon got the hint that maybe the excuses she gave were just that, excuses.

I tried a younger, high school age girl. She played with all the kids, and actually had the boys asking for her to come back. That's unusual, because they would rather be on their own at home whenever possible. Her name and number were moved to the top of the list, and things went fairly smooth until her school activities kept her busy, which left her with little time for babysitting. She didn't even charge a lot. Her reason was that Lisa didn't have any serious medical problems, like being on a monitor or needing tube feedings. Thank goodness for that. According to the sitter, Lisa had Down syndrome and a heart problem; but otherwise, it was no big deal!

The next person we tried was a mother herself, and she sometimes brought her own children to our house when we needed her. She was able to babysit during the day, when I sometimes had trouble getting someone to watch Lisa. She worked out well. At some point in time, she asked to watch the kids in her home, which also worked out. We came to a mutual agreement, without the Respite coordinator being involved. I didn't have to pay this caretaker as much as normal, because we agreed on a specific hourly rate. She was really great with Lisa, and we ended up using her exclusively. She treated Lisa like one of her own, and always included Lisa whenever she had fun activities planned with her own children. It was good for Lisa, because she got out of our house a little more often, and learned some good social skills being around other kids.

I can thank the Respite program for finding and training this caregiver, and I thank the caregiver for going above and beyond what was necessary to help us out. The Respite program had its ups and downs, and I'm not sure if it's still in operation today. There was always funding concerns, and finding the right kind of people to fill the caretaker role. It's never easy finding childcare for a child with a disability, especially if there are severe physical or medical problems. The Respite program filled a need in the community, and I hope a lot of parents and children benefitted. I am grateful for their service, and hope that they are still providing services in some capacity. You never know when you are going to need something like this. It's definitely a relief for us parents.

Sister as a Babysitter

When Lisa was born, she had a sister who was seven and a half years old and two brothers, one who was two years old and the other who was three and a half years old. They were anxious to have their baby sister home, and oohed and aahed over her a lot. Of course, the first thing they all wanted to do was hold her. They each took a turn sitting at one end of the couch, holding their new baby sister. They propped one arm on the couch's arm rest, cradled Lisa's head, and then held the rest of her with the other arm wrapped around her legs and stomach. The two older children just looked at her and touched her hands gently. The two year old went straight for the head, patting the cheeks, rubbing her almost baldhead, and tried to touch every part of her face. He was gentle but curious. Maybe he realized that this was the new baby, and he had just moved up from that position to being the older brother and "a big boy."

They were all excited to have a chance to hold her, and they were good to her, but the newness was short lived. Pretty soon, the boys were off to playing with their trucks and blocks and big sister had her day planner filled with activities with friends. It was the end of spring, the end of school and the beginning of summer. No time for a baby. The kids did help when I needed someone to do a diaper or bottle run. They knew to grab the extras as well, such as clean plastic pants, maybe some new large diaper pins or ointment. They also got pretty good at warming the bottle under warm water and testing it on the wrist. What a great group!

There came a time when Lisa was a few months old, and we needed a sitter. I had several regulars before she was born, but hadn't used anyone since her birth. When I called them for this upcoming evening, I felt obligated, no, let's say compelled, to tell them Lisa had Down syndrome. I don't believe any of them ever shied away from babysitting because of Lisa, so we didn't have any trouble getting someone. But I had trouble leaving her with anyone. I still worried about her health, though I knew there was no life threatening or any immediate health dangers. I tried to get some of the older high school babysitters, because I thought they would do better. It didn't turn out that way.

There were several incidents that made me take a good, long look at who was actually doing the "sitting" and who was doing the baby care. My husband and I went out one night, and I received a call from our oldest daughter. She said she was calling about Lisa. I don't remember the exact conversation but she must have been concerned that Lisa was not eating, sleeping or something because she normally would wait until we got home to tell us anything that may have happened while we were gone. The next day, I talked to our oldest some more about the call, and found out that *she* (not the sitter) was the one who changed Lisa's diapers, gave her a bottle and put her to bed. The so-called sitter was on the phone or watching television during the time that our daughter was caring for Lisa's needs. At this point that is when I decided to let Lisa's sister do the babysitting. I think we said we'd pay her, but I'm sure she probably got short-changed a lot of times. Usually we'd leave her for only a couple hours, and at first I'd worry about how young she was. She was younger than most sitters I had hired up till now, but she was more responsible than a lot of high school kids. I was also concerned with how this would affect her attitude towards Lisa at that time, and in the future. I didn't want our oldest to ever feel obligated to care for Lisa; ever. I didn't want her to grow to hate Lisa for being the baby, for having a disability, for being spoiled or any other reason siblings use to come to hate each other.

    I was certain if there were any major problems with all this, it would be with her "having" to babysit for her brothers and sister. We never told her she couldn't do something just because we wanted to have her babysit instead. Most of the time I tried to ask her ahead of time. We also had other sitters, which meant that she wasn't always the one in charge. And we really didn't go out much when the kids were younger. Finances were tight raising four children, and me being a stay at home mom didn't bring in any income. But, I believe it was a positive experience for everyone. Lisa's sister and her brothers have all formed compassion for others and want to help those less fortunate people. They are not afraid to be around people with disabilities, and have volunteered to help in many fundraiser activities that involve and include people with disabilities. I don't believe any of them are embarrassed to have Lisa as their sister. The opposite is probably more accurate. Having Lisa around actually helped them to strike up conversations with that one girl or guy they wanted to meet. And Lisa was always a good excuse when they wanted to go to a kid's movie without seeming like a little kid themselves. She was also an excuse when they *didn't* want to go somewhere. They might be talking to a not-so-liked classmate who would want to plan something, and occasionally one of Lisa's siblings would say, "No, I can't go. I have to babysit."

I always said I wouldn't ask any of them to consider caring for her after we're dead and gone, but was glad when our oldest daughter and her husband broached the subject, asking to be listed as a guardian or caretaker. How appropriate and heartwarming to think of an older sister who babysat for Lisa many years ago would now ask to care for her in her later years. I just hope I don't have to pay by the hour!

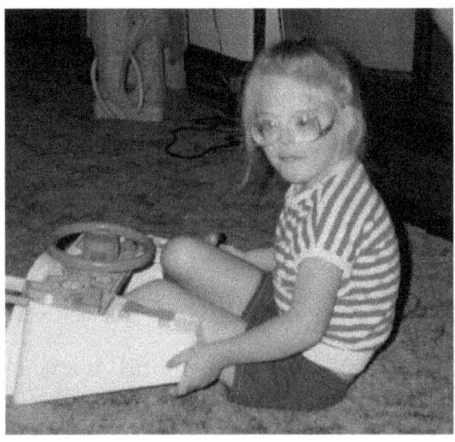

"She Ain't Heavy, Mom. She's My Sister."

The noise level in the living room rises. Voices get nasty and louder. Threats of "I'm telling mom" are quickly followed by "I hate you. I wish you weren't my sister (or brother)." This happened at our house on occasions when the kids disagreed or were at odds with each other. I usually tried to stay out of it, hoping those who were arguing could solve it by themselves. I do remember that I intervened for Lisa, thinking she could not stand up to the verbal abuse of her siblings or be able to defend herself. I was also afraid that the siblings would say they hate her, and I surely didn't want Lisa to think that could be possible. I was concerned with the fact that because she had Down syndrome, she might think this was the cause for their dislike of her.

Boy, was I wrong. The brothers and sisters could fight with each other, yelling awful insinuations and pledge life-long promises, only to be found together later on as thick as thieves. Siblings fight, siblings love, and siblings are together forever, no matter what. But what do they think of each other, especially of one who has a disability? I asked Lisa's siblings how they felt, having a sister with Down syndrome, and their comeback was, "We are the only ones on the block who have a sister with Down syndrome."

I remember when my husband and I sat down with our three oldest, wondering how to tell them their newborn sister had a disability. They all listened intently and made no comments until I finished telling about Down syndrome, about it's characteristics and about any problems associated with Down syndrome. Our oldest was seven and a half at the time, and handled the information in a very mature manner. Her response to me was "If retarded means slow, then it will just take Lisa longer to learn." If I had dry eyes up to this point in the conversation, that statement made my eyes well up with tears.

How could someone so young be so grown up in this situation? She took the information in stride, acting as if everyone had someone with a disability in his or her family. The two boys were much smaller and only knew their little sister would not be sharing their room, which made them very happy. They all helped with Lisa and never acted ashamed or embarrassed by her uniqueness. Lisa was a part of the family, going and doing the same activities as that of the other children. In her early years, there were some minor problems that surfaced which concerned me. When strangers asked her age, the boys sometimes said she was younger. I asked why they would tell someone she was two when she was actually four. One of her brothers answered that it was easier to make her younger then to explain why she couldn't ride a tricycle or do the same kinds of things four year olds do.

While Lisa's brothers and sister made allowances for her to make her look better, they never said they hated her because she had Down syndrome. They also verbalized that they were not ashamed of her. Embarrassed, yes, when she would drool grape juice down her shirt after gargling with it or when she used a new word that was not acceptable in public, but ashamed, nope. And what if they were? Could I do anything to change that? NO. Life is not always fair, and we all must cope with different problems and obstacles. Lisa has had to cope with others teasing and making fun of her, but from the first incident, we taught her how to handle those frustrating times. She learned to tell those who call her retarded that it just means slow, and she can learn as well as anyone. She learned that if the teasing continued, she should go find an adult to help her handle the situation. She added her own self-defense approach by saying if someone called her names or bothered her in some unacceptable way she would "Kick them in the #!&@#." Now, I did not encourage this, but if she felt the urge, I might have chosen to turn and look the other way and not to see this demonstration in action. I was not condoning the deed, but I could understand it if that would have been her way to handle the conflict.

I asked the children what specific things they could recall that had a negative impact on them when it came to Lisa. They said they did not like being told by adults that they were special to have a sister like Lisa. They figured having a fourth child in any family was not special, just crowded. They also said that they did not like the stares and negative comments about Lisa. According to them, Lisa didn't look any different, so why were people being so rude. Family ties sometimes make us blind to our deficiencies, thank goodness. I also asked what comments or gestures made them feel good about Lisa. Such things as treating her like any other child and seeing adults being helpful in stressful situations were their answers. They agreed that no words could ever change Lisa, but they wanted others to know they could help by listening. The siblings also agreed they had accepted Lisa for who she was, what she could become, and that they loved her without reservations. Like one brother said as he carried her up some steps one day, "She ain't heavy, mom, she's my sister."

Lisa may always be the brunt of teasing and jokes, because some people are not mature enough to see past the disability. She has had to learn to cope with these aggravations and go on with her life. As a family, we have had to learn to cope with the taunts and stares and get past it. Sometimes it was difficult to know how to handle the various situations. We were not handed a book when Lisa was born, yet we learned to deal with and learn about her as we all experienced new incidents. It is the same with siblings, learning to accept her as she is and be proud to have her as a sister.

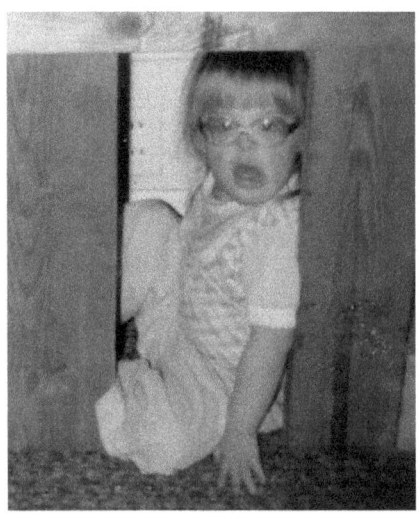

Setting Child Free Isn't Easy for Mom

There are many modes of transportation for children, and Lisa has definitely had her share. She has probably extended their use longer than most kids, simply because she did not out grow them very quickly. Her first vehicle was the stroller. This was during the "umbrella" era, and that's what we used for Lisa, a red umbrella stroller. During this era, no one we knew owned a fancy, heavy-duty stroller with the fringe on the top. Nor did anyone we know have a big buggy carrier that had room for six or was able to convert it to either sitting or sleeping areas as needed.

No, we owned a modified version of a sling-back infant seat on wheels, which folded up easily. It could hang on a small hook in the closet when not used by either the child or a child's baby doll. This stroller doubled as a play stroller for Lisa's older sister's baby dolls for a long time.

Lisa was able to use this stroller quite a bit longer than most, because of her short, petite stature. I remember walking her to preschool, pushing her in the red and white-checkered stroller, taking in the surrounding sights and sounds, unaware that others her age would be walking to preschool. This was also the first of many times I would ignore the obvious warning label many items had attached to them. You know, the "Do not use for children over the age of three" (four, five or whatever age the company decides is too old for a specific item). With Lisa, age made no difference, only her size did.

At the age when other youngsters were learning to walk, Lisa was still learning to crawl. When others were testing their new tennis shoes in the mud and water, Lisa was trying to make sure her shoes were flat and on steady ground for stability. And, as children her age were busy motivating a new scooter without pedals, or using that first big wheel, Lisa was learning to walk on carpet.

Besides, she had a big disadvantage when it came to tricycles and big wheels. Her legs were too short. I realized that she probably knew what to do, because she tried awfully hard to make things move, but it took her a lot longer to master anything because of the length of her legs. We put pedal extenders on the tricycle, but had no real success for several years.

Finally, at an age when I thought she should be riding a bike, she mastered the tricycle and big wheel. The first few tries were about the same. Pedal a little, readjust her sitting position, pout or cry until somebody helped, then quickly get off. The pouting usually worked, but one day I finally told her to keep trying and I bravely walked into the house to let her work on pedaling.

She must have done something right, because I couldn't find her when I went back outside a couple of minutes later. Talk about panic! I looked up and down the sidewalk, in three different directions, hollered at the neighborhood kids to help look for her and felt my heart rate quickly increase. I finally saw her at the far end of the block. There she came, pedaling for all she's worth, laughing and smiling. She was finally mobile, finally free.

That was short-lived, because I soon imposed boundaries for her. She did not like learning about these restrictions. The last time she took off, the third time in that day, I found her half way to our neighborhood school, "to play on the toys." This sounded innocent enough, but I knew better than to let those big blue eyes and wavering voice get to me. Home we marched, where she was confined to the yard.

It was hard to give her the freedom she needed, to let her explore so she could grow to be carefree and independent. Just letting her outside without supervision was a big step for me. I was learning, just as Lisa did with her advancements from walking to tricycle and big wheel riding. I've taken one step at a time, relaxed some of her boundary restrictions and readjusted my viewpoint, to look at her as a growing and independent person.

I would watch her grow and go, but I also tried to hold on a little longer, keep her as my baby and maybe subconsciously hope she would need me for several years. I soon realized that was not fair to her. I would try to be realistic about the newfound freedom she loved so much. We were both learning.

The Birthday Bike

Lisa asked for two things for her birthday, a bike and a flashlight. The bike for obvious reasons; she did not own one. The flashlight was a different matter. She explained to me that her bike would probably be hiding under our bed, and the flashlight would come in handy when she had to look for it. She also said she would use the flashlight at night when she wanted to read while in bed, under the covers no less!

On the day of her 9th birthday, she invited a neighbor friend over for cake, ice cream and to watch her open her presents. The flashlight was first. She was real excited to see that. As I was trying to decide how to give her the bike, she took the flashlight and headed for my bedroom with her friend close behind. It was a comical sight, watching her get down on her hands and knees and then to a prone position. Her friend did the same, though she had a puzzled look on her face. Lisa turned on the flashlight and directed the beam under the bed, while she used the other hand to lift up the quilted spread. She looked all over, first from one side and then from the other. In the meantime, her dad brought the bike to the dining room from its basement-hiding place. As Lisa was looking in the other room, he set the bike up near the table to await her return. After several minutes, she and her friend stood up in dismay. Lisa said something like "Maybe it's upstairs under *my* bed." I couldn't understand why she would think it could fit under any bed at all. I had to do some fast-talking to convince her that maybe she should just give up the hunt. While walking back to the dining room, she was looking down at her flashlight, trying to figure out how to turn it off. She rounded the corner, and almost fell on top of her new bike. She looked at it in a startled way, and calmly said, "Oh, there it is," as if she simply misplaced it.

There it was; a shiny, new pink bike with streamers of pink and white flowing from the ends of the white gripped handles. The seat was small and contoured, not the long banana shape that were popular and on some bikes. There was a horn on the handlebars, and a pink swirly design on the front and back rims that covered the tires. This was Lisa's birthday bike, and when she saw it she immediately climbed on. As she tried to push herself up onto the seat, which was adjusted too high, she felt the bike slightly move. As quickly as she had jumped on, she jumped off. I started to talk fast, hopefully to get her back on the bike unafraid. I showed her the bonus features on the bike. It had two little circular objects attached to either side of the back tires. You guessed it, training wheels.

Yes, this is a little strange, but let me explain. First of all, how many nine year olds get a 12" bike? Most children that age usually receive a 16," 20" or 24" bike. The other strange thing about this *was* the training wheels. You have to remember that Lisa has always had slow development in her gross motor skills. She only mastered a tricycle after riding one for several summers. She was not much for being outdoors, or moving about by means of something other than her own two feet. She tried the various modes of transportation for children, but with measured success.

We decided to take the new bike outside because I thought it would be easier for her to ride where having a smooth sidewalk could ease the movement. Carpet is always very hard to pedal over. I was wrong about going outside. Our sidewalk was definitely not smooth. There were raised areas at the ends of certain sections of the cement or there are pieces of sidewalk missing. This made bike riding difficult, especially the first time. After a lot of talking on my part, and only one-word sentences such as "No" from Lisa, I finally got her to try. She got on, slowly sat on the seat and tried to reach the pedals. Once again, her short legs did not reach. Time out to readjust. The seat was adjusted to a lower position, and she gingerly climbed back on.

We now started at the cross section of the sidewalk, headed towards a neighbor's house. She finally began to pedal, slowly but surely. Then we discovered another problem. The training wheels were slightly higher than the larger back wheel, and this made the bike wobble from side to side. Sure enough, the wobbling made her holler again. After several attempts to move, which caused a wobble each time, Lisa gave up. Another adjustment, another locker room talk, another try. Now she sat there, feet firmly placed on the pedals, and hollered, "I can't move. I'm stuck!" The front wheel was up against a bump in the walk, and she had no strength to pedal up and over it. After a little help, she made it and was headed down the walk.

I thought she was going a little fast when I noticed her feet no longer kept up with the pedals. She yelled for help, the bike kept moving and another problem suddenly developed. She couldn't stop. No one had explained how to brake the pedals. There she went, straight for a tree, her legs spread out in a 180-degree horizontal line. She hit that tree dead on, as if she had closely calculated this maneuver. She was not seriously hurt, though this took some more fast-talking on my part to convince her of that. On her next try, she did fairly well, though she didn't last too long. She complained of tired legs and wanting to do something else. I'm sure Lisa was also tired of saying WHOA, because she still hadn't figured out how to brake. I guess she thought her voice command would do the trick. Needless to say, the bike did not get worn out that summer. It spent a lot of time in the garage.

Lo and behold, the next summer was different. She asked for it one day when she saw her neighbor friend riding a bike. We got Lisa's bike out of its' storage space in the garage and she hopped right on. Another surprising fact was she could pedal faster and turn corners without stopping. The best thing of all was that somehow she learned how to brake and stop the bike. An additional nice little extra was the fact that she was too tall for the lowered seat. We had to adjust it up, and that was a first for any of her former modes of wheeled transportation. Now she traveled the sidewalks, while her friend rode the streets. She was limited to the end of the block either way from our house and was not allowed to go any further. I became very uncomfortable when she turned a corner and headed down the walk out of sight. She wanted to ride her bike to school in the fall, but we had a ways to go before we got to that point. I mean really, have you even seen a fourth grader ride a small, 12" bicycle to school, with training wheels?

SNAPSHOTS OF LISA

Christmas Program

Every year I went through the same routine for the annual school Christmas program. I would help Lisa pick out a special dress to wear, complete with the matching red or white tights, shiny black dress shoes and ribbons or bows in her hair. Lisa always complained that the shoes pinched, the dress was too tight and the tights were way too big. Nevertheless, she would dress herself hours before the necessary time and then sat quietly on the couch singing the selected Christmas songs that her class had been practicing for weeks.

When it was time to leave for the school, she would holler "I don't want to step in the snow and get my shoes wet." Her Dad also thought she should be carried so she wouldn't slip. "Those soles are as smooth as glass." Consequently, Lisa was usually carried to the car on her Christmas program night, at least during her younger years.

When we arrived at the school, we let Lisa lead us to her room, even though we really knew where it was. We always tried to encourage that independence thing. She felt good about finding her room, and we could only hope that this insignificant accomplishment might help her in the future. We left her with the teacher and fellow students, and headed for the gym to find the best seat possible, like all the other excited and proud parents.

One particular Christmas though, I was not sure I would ever want to see my child on stage again. I knew things like this happened, but I was not ready to admit she was mine when she became a stage "star" at the young age of four. As her class walked on stage, Lisa lagged behind because of steps she had to climb. She held onto the rail with her left hand and her dress with her right. I still don't know why she had to hold on to her dress, because it wasn't floor length, but she must have felt that it was important to do so. Maybe she was practicing to be a runway model.

Even her teacher tried to get Lisa to release her right hand from the hem of her dress, but Lisa held tight. I didn't really like to see her slip showing as she walked up and onto the stage, but I figured it was better than seeing more than just a slip. Little did I know what was to come next. She made it to the top of the steps, placed one foot onto the stage, and tripped. She did not fall down, but tumbled forward into the next person, who did fall down. Lisa also let go of her dress, which was probably a good thing.

She began her walk across the stage and had to step across several cords that were hooked up to the microphones. I thought she did rather well, having to look down before stepping over these and walk at the same time. Her depth perception was not good, and because of this she would usually stop, look down and then move cautiously forward. She arrived at her designated spot, faced the audience, and turned to get situated in her place, which included bumping into the child next to her again. That young boy quickly turned and wacked Lisa a good one in the arm. At that point, I thought we would all hear her famous yell, but she just looked at him like he was from outer space.

The children were finally settled and ready to sing. Their classroom teacher was in the wings in case of trouble while the music teacher took her place in front of the stage to direct these lovely children. The boy on Lisa's left had a nice, red bow tie on and he began to fidget with it nervously. Lisa leaned over to help him adjust it, then quietly said something that made him quit messing with his bow tie.

It was time for the music to start, which coincided with Lisa's act. She stole the show. Because she was significantly shorter than most of her classmates, she was in the front row. I am sure this was definitely contributory to being able to steal the show. She began to mouth the words in time to the music, but I knew full well that she was not really singing. She was preoccupied with her attire, busy arranging the ruffles on her dress and pressing her hands down the front, as if they were a heated iron. When this action was completed to her satisfaction, she focused her attention on her tights. This was the showstopper and made her into the star of the program.

Her obvious first plan was to pull the tights up at the waist. You could see this did not work, even with all her wiggling. The excess material still hung loosely around the ankles. She bent over at the waist, reached down to her ankles and slowly grasped the material. Inch by inch, she stretched those tights, pulled them towards her knees, ever-so-slowly to her waist. Yes, to her waist. And all this time she was lip-syncing! As she pulled the tights up, her dress came up as well and she was now considered the youngest exhibitionist on stage. She did this not once, but twice, once for each leg. I thought I would turn ten shades of red, but no one noticed me. All eyes were on Lisa. She was oblivious to the snickers and giggles from the audience, because she was too busy straightening and adjusting her tights. I never did hear a word of singing from Lisa. I was too busy watching her and tried to catch her attention in the hopes that she would stop her fussing. I began to wave my arms wildly, and probably attracted more attention than Lisa was getting at that moment. I soon decided she was not going to see or hear me, so I sat down quietly. Besides, I really did not want anyone to know that she and I were related. I did see my daughter as she innocently finished her adjustments, took a bow with the other students, and slowly began her walk across the stage towards the steps. As a last gesture, she stopped, turned towards the audience, bowed again, waved, smiled, and continued off stage, to cookies and punch. What a night to remember!

Sleep Habit Techniques of Lisa

When Lisa was a baby, her sleep habits were quickly formed. At first, all she did was eat and sleep, sleep and eat. Of course, if she slept more than four hours at a time, I was in the room, making sure I could still hear her breathe or feel her move. A lot of times I would actually slip my hand under the pink receiving blanket and feel her chest rise with each breath, just to be sure.

She spent her first three months in a bassinette and was bothered nightly by me. I just wanted to be sure she was okay. She was later moved to a port-a-crib instead of a normal sized crib, because I read somewhere that babies who slept in small spaces experienced a close, secure feeling, which was good for them.

She must have sensed that, for when I later moved her to the larger sleeping quarters, she began to wake *me* up. I guess she was just checking to make sure that I was close by. Her sleep habits were also disturbed by numerous ear infections. This meant neither one of us got a full nights' sleep for quite a few months.

When she would be sick with pneumonia, bronchitis or croup, I had her sleep on a couch in the living room, which was near our bedroom. It seemed easier at the time, instead of me walking up and down those 18 steps to the second floor, four times a night. For these times, I jokingly made a "bed" for her on the couch, not knowing that she would take it seriously.

Whenever any of my kids took sick, I felt more comfortable knowing they were close by me, without actually being in the same bed or room with me at nighttime. The living room couch was ideal. I guess I thought I should hear the child toss and turn, moan and groan, and call out for yet "one more drink, please." Lisa was no exception. The nights were long on time and we were short on sleep.

As her health improved, I would try to move her back to her own bed upstairs. This did not work out well and most nights she would end up back on the couch. Sometimes this would happen even after several attempts of bribing to get her to stay in her own bed. If it got to the point where her crying and whining kept me awake (which was usually the case), I would go up, get her out of bed, and make her "bed" on the couch. I was a pushover, and she was a pro.

Because she was mobile, I would often fall asleep thinking she would spend the night in her bed, only to wake up in the morning and find her sleeping peacefully on the couch. This was a difficult habit to break, but we finally managed to do so, with the help of a new couch. The rule was "No one can sleep on the couch." It worked, and I wished I had thought of it earlier, even though it was an expensive solution. It also made Dad unhappy as well; no more naps on the couch during a football game.

When Lisa started school, her bedtime was around 8 p.m. The nightly ritual usually included finding a stuffed animal to sleep with, making sure her pillow was straight, read a book, having me say her prayers to her, with her repeating them to me, giving goodnight hugs and kisses, saying "Good-night, sleep tight, don't let the bedbugs bite" and last but not least, the most famous stall, a drink of water. Try to do all that in five minutes or less!

After that, there was the phase of getting up in the middle of the night to go to the bathroom. I could almost set my clock by her nightly trips downstairs. It's funny how she passed the upstairs bathroom, never once thinking she could go all by herself without waking me. The routine was always the same. First, I heard the sound of this little person scooting down the stairs on her bottom with a bump, bump, bump. She would stop at the third or fourth step from the bottom and quietly awaken me with "Mommy, I have to go potty."

Ignoring her was not the answer. Trying to encourage her to go by herself did not work well either. Her complaint was "It's too dark, I can't see." I could never figure out how she got from her room, through the hall and down the flight of stairs if it was too dark. I stumbled and grumbled, got her taken care of and took her back up to bed. Lisa would wait until I was out of her bedroom and I was on my way downstairs to my own room, before I would here her whisper "I need a drink of water." I thought this might work against me later, if I would again have to repeat the nighttime bathroom ritual, but I usually honored her request, and hoped she would not wake until morning.

Getting her to stay in her bed at night was an ongoing feat, but not nearly as difficult as getting her up in the morning. She had the same excuses her sister and brothers used for not getting up. The usually lines include "Go away…wake up someone else," "I'm not going to school today," and "I'm too tired."

For my newest technique, I used a kitchen timer. I woke up Lisa, making sure she could answer my questions coherently. I set the timer for five minutes. If she was out of bed before it went off, she collected 50 cents. My boys had a fit when they found out I was paying her to get up in the morning. I explained why this had to be done, hoping to slowly decrease the reward as she learned to get out of bed when first called. My other hope was that the boys continued to wake up on their own, or it could have turned into a real expensive lesson for ME!

A Piercing Experience for Mom and Daughter

Lisa was seven when she first talked of having her ears pierced. Lisa must have been inspired by her older sister's variety of earrings and the two holes she had in each lobe. Lisa talked for hours about getting matching earrings for her favorite outfits, and wondered whether to buy the pink and green striped mini-bows or the purple pig earrings. Such decisions and she didn't have them pierced yet. I also agreed that it would be nice for her to get her ears pierced and encouraged her to talk about it as much as possible. She really got carried away with it at times and I soon came to regret my enthusiastic encouragement.

Every time we passed a jewelry counter she would stop and look at the big selection, always hollering for me to look at her most favorite pair that week. She was either going to own a lot of earrings or she kept changing her favorite color and style, depending on the day and her mood. It may have also had something to do with her outfit she was wearing at the time, for her choice for that day seemed to match the outfit she had on.

I spent a lot of time talking about what would have to be done in order to get her ears pierced. I even talked about that steel, silver piece of equipment that looked like a gun, and the step-by-step procedure for getting the ears pierced. I did try to downplay the actual piercing because I didn't really want to scare her. I talked about the after care, turning the posts and cleansing them daily to insure nicely healed lobes. I talked about how she'd have to wait six weeks at least (a long, long time for her) before she could change the earrings. I wasn't trying to discourage this popular trend that most girls want at some point in time, but I did want her to know all that goes along with having pierced ears.

As her eighth birthday approached, she became more excited about having two more holes in her head; you know, in addition to ears, mouth and nostrils. She was delighted to open all the birthday cards that came in the mail and find folding money that came with some of those cards. She had decided that the folding money would be saved to get her ears pierced. But any coins she acquired were to be readily spent on pop, candy and other treats. I guess she thought the change would not be as easy to keep as the dollar bills. Or was it because the change would be too heavy for the envelope she had marked "Pierced Ears" money?

Our trips to the mall took us past the earring store, which sparked conversation on the subject of ears. Walking by jewelry counters in other stores would cause us to delay our destination arrival while Lisa ooohed and aaahed at the variety of earrings. It seemed like everything centered on earrings at this point in time. I was getting impatient and I'm sure Lisa felt the same. Finally, the big day arrived.

We celebrated her birthday, took the money she had saved and went to get the "greatest present ever." (According to Lisa, anyway). Would you believe she never stepped inside the store that day to get her ears pierced? She backed away from the doorway by saying she really didn't like things on her ears. I tried to talk to her about it, hoping she might reconsider her sudden change of attitude, but nothing I said would modify her decision. We left the store that day empty-handed, but she bought herself a special food treat and something from the toy store instead. No more was mentioned for about a year, until her birthday came around again. Out of the blue, she announced her intention to have her ears pierced on this birthday. I said I wouldn't discuss it at length (I'd done that routine before) and insisted she make her decision quickly. I once again explained the procedure and follow-up treatment. She was still agreeable and somewhat insistent about doing it this time, "for sure."

When we arrived at the store, Lisa eagerly sought out the sales clerk and told the nice young lady what she planned. The sales clerk was very nice and patient, thank goodness. She listened to Lisa's version of the procedure and reiterated the same information with some additions or corrections. Lisa climbed up onto the high stool, wrapped her legs around the silver leg supports and waited.

First came the measuring and markings on Lisa's ear lobes for perfectly placed holes. The blue marker made a small dot in the exact intended spot, and I approved the position on each ear lobe. My only thought was they had better do the two lobes at the same time or the second lobe would never get pierced.

The clerk must have been a mind reader, for she soon called someone over to help her. Once more I gave a quick pep talk to Lisa, then there was a "gun" to each lobe, directions for Lisa to take a deep breath, and zap, zap, she had a hole in each of her ear lobes. She looked a little startled, yet slowly a smile spread across her face. "I did it, I did it." That's about all she could say.

We let her look in the mirror, and listened once again to the care and cleaning directions. Lisa needed help getting down from the tall stool, and she seemed a little unstable with her walking at first.

Once we got out of the store, she looked at me with tears in her eyes and said "They sting and feel hot." Her lobes were red and slightly swollen, but nothing out of the ordinary.

I asked her if she was crying because they hurt. She said no, she was just so happy to have her ears pierced and "The tears just dripped out." Waiting a year, and letting her do it by her own choice was the easiest way for both of us.

The Neighborhood School was a Great Choice

When Lisa reached school age, Lisa and other children with disabilities were guaranteed a free appropriate public education according to public law 94-142. State and local governments are still required to provide programs that identify all children with disabilities, give each child an education that is specific to the child's needs, and provide other services as needed to help the child.

Along with the free appropriate education, it must be in the least restrictive environment. This is what led us to decide on a change of schools for Lisa. Before Lisa changed schools, we realized she needed friends. It was not enough to just have acquaintances in her special education classroom. They were her friends during school hours but when they were bused to their homes in neighborhoods and other towns, the social aspect stopped. Lisa had no friends in our neighborhood. She needed friends to grow, mature and become an independent adult.

There were a lot of people involved in making the decision to have Lisa go to our neighborhood school and it took a combined effort from many to make it work, but it was worth it. We made countless preparations, had many meetings and talked about the transition a lot. As a result, Lisa's first two years attending a regular education classroom created many positive changes in her life.

One final meeting before her transition to the neighborhood school sticks in my mind because of the impact it had on others in attendance that day. The principal of the grade school asked Lisa's Dad what he actually expected or hoped for by having Lisa attend the neighborhood school. My husband had a very serious look when he said, "I want her to function at the appropriate fourth-grade level."

Here was this 10-year-old girl with Down syndrome who could barely read or do math past a first or second grade level, and he was telling the principal this! I could see right away what he was getting at, but the principal didn't have a clue. Her jaw dropped and I'm sure she thought we were both loony to expect this grade school to bring Lisa up to grade level in academics.

My husband's next comment helped to cleared up the first. He said that's what he would like, but he knew it was not possible. What he could see happening was Lisa interacting with children her own age, appropriate placement for learning proper social skills and their acceptance of her as an equal. We realized Lisa might never be as academically inclined as we would hope, but we wanted her to have the same opportunities as her peers. She needed to develop independent skills to survive in this world.

We continued to work with the school to prepare for her entry in the fall. Fortunately, the educators listened to our comments and requests, and recognized our feelings about this placement. Parents are important in decisions such as this. Who else knows the child better than the parents? Thank goodness the principal and other teachers had enough faith in their own teaching abilities and enough compassion in their hearts to welcome Lisa without causing a lot of hubbub. They were willing to give it a worthwhile try.

Lisa began to change quite quickly, from when she first started in her neighborhood school to when she got settled into a routine. I could see she was more confident and self-assured. She was happy in a classroom with kids her age, had made many friends and continued to improve her skills in her schoolwork. Regular classes were encouraged, with anticipated improvements, though this was definitely not a major factor when making the decision for Lisa to change schools.

Lisa was not the only one who benefited from this change. Those children who got to know her were better able to accept others for their differences and respect all people, regardless of their capabilities. Those children were also the same people who would undoubtedly hire her as an adult.

By going to school with Lisa and getting to know her as a person, her classmates could judge her on her merit and not on her unjust label of having a disability. They would see what she could do, not what she could not do. I hoped the teachers would also benefit from having Lisa in the building by realizing a person should not be judged by a label but by their abilities. All children have different abilities and need to be recognized this way. We are all individuals with the same needs and desires.

I applaud those teachers who worked with Lisa, those who were in the special education classrooms as well as those teachers in regular education classes who taught Lisa without the benefit of special education training. I am sure one fear the educators felt was in not knowing how to teach Lisa, because of her disability. I could understand this feeling, but with guidance and reassurance those fears soon subsided.

When Lisa was born, we were not given any formal training or a book on how to deal with the disability. We simply learned, one day at a time. If there had been someone there in the delivery room to give training sessions, I think the following would be included, as it should be with any child.

1. Expect the best from her and she will respond.

2. Treat her with respect and as an individual.

3. Answer the many questions that others have, to dispel any myths they may have unjustly formed against her.

4. Perhaps most important: love her.

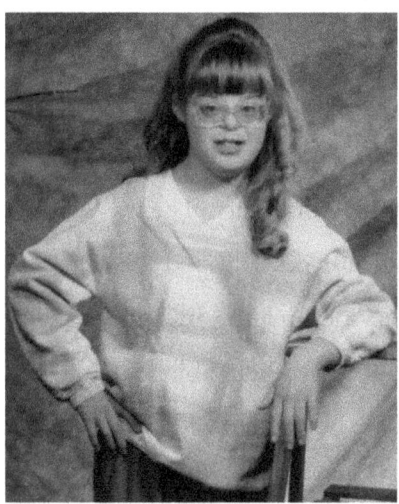

Going to the Neighborhood School: A Positive Step

From the beginning, Lisa's first grade school experiences had always been in a special classroom for children who need extra help. One year, we decided to try a different option and chose to have Lisa go to her "neighborhood" school, meaning the same school that her brothers and sister attended. She continued at the same school again the following two years, but that first year proved to be a challenging step for Lisa. It was also a big adjustment for all of us.

I was nervous; Lisa was very excited. She was finally going to attend school with the kids from our neighborhood, walk to school with them, play with them and hopefully make new friends. My worries included her having to adjust to a new building layout, the teachers and the children. Would she adjust to all these changes and continue to love school, or would she come home scared and upset?

My fears were calmed on that first day when Lisa and I talked after school. I asked how her day was, and she burst out excitedly with the information, "Mom, I got a science book!" To her, it was like winning a shopping spree at a toy store. She went on to describe her science class and all those bugs and stuff that really thrilled her. Later on, she had even collected some of those "lovely" bugs. The first time she showed me a lifeless creature lying in the palm of her hand, I made her throw it down. She put up a fuss, showed me her sad face and insisted it was for science. I reluctantly agreed she could pick it up and keep it in a jar with the lid on.

Lisa adjusted to her new and varied school schedule rather quickly, knowing when she should to go to her resource reading and math classes, as well as PE, music and lunch. She dawdled at times in a hallway or in the bathroom, which caused concern with some of the teachers. They would sound a silent "Lisa alert" and had a fellow student follow her designated route. They always found her (thank goodness) usually en route and in low gear. More power to the staff if they could find another speed for Lisa; I had been trying to get her to move a little faster for years.

Lisa spent half her day in the regular fourth grade classroom, and worked with the class in science and social studies. She had lots of helpers, and the teacher included Lisa in as many activities as possible. She attended a regular PE class, which gave her a chance to compete with others her age. Her size and capabilities were noticeably different, but with help and adaptations from the teacher, she was challenged in her physical abilities. In music, she sang right along with all the other children. She had good rhythm and could carry a recognizable tune. She was able to do many things we had worked on and a few things we were not expecting. She adjusted well to all the situations.

There was one curious incident we did not foresee. A former classmate of Lisa's at the special education classroom across town was having trouble adjusting to the new school year without Lisa being presence in his room. He and Lisa had been classmates for several years. Lisa's former DLP,[10] or Development Learning Program teacher made a special effort to alleviate his concern when the problem became apparent. The teacher arranged a time for Lisa to visit her "old" school and friends. She had lunch there and reassured everyone that her "new" school was okay, and so was she. What a twist to the kinds of adjustments everyone had made. Lisa adjusted and I truly believe, for her needs, she was in the best school possible. This was not the only unexpected incidence that happened because of Lisa's new school placement.

Another unforeseen outcome happened one morning, as I dropped Lisa off at the sitter's house, which was a block away from her elementary school. She seemed to skip all the usual habits we had established in the car. You know, things like "Bye," or "Have a good day," or "See you after school," or "I love you," as well as the hugs, kisses and encouragements. It was usually like going to bed at night. She liked to drag it out as long as possible. This specific morning, she opened the door almost as soon as I pulled into the driveway, jumped out and waved, and quickly walked toward the house. As she reached the green screen door of the screened-in porch, I slowly backed out into the street to drive away. I glanced up in time to see her walk back down the steps. I stopped, rolled down the window, and told her to go onto the front porch and into the house. She slowly walked back up the steps and went inside the screen door. I thought she was headed for their main door, so I again started down the street.

When I reached the corner, I glanced back just in time to see that green screen door opening slowly. I quickly drove around the block and pulled to an immediate halt just in time to see her starting across the street toward school. I jumped out of the car, and headed straight toward her displaying my mad face. Lisa took one look at me, dropped her lower jaw, made a quick turn and did double-time back to the sitter's house. I stopped her long enough to talk to her and explain it was too early to go to school. She hesitantly agreed, and went into the sitter's house on her own. Her actions made me stop and think that just maybe she wanted to do it all by herself, to prove her capabilities and be given the independence she so deserves. Lisa became more self-assured and independent and, even though I may not have liked what she tried, I was pleased that she constantly tested her abilities and stretched her boundaries.

My hope for Lisa was to gain advancement in her social skills so she could make friends with those around her and be accepted without judgment. I always thought that the children she associated during her early years with would someday be the adults who hire her in the community. For Lisa, the neighborhood school concept was a positive step in her future.

The Dreaded IEP

Any parent who has a child with a disability knows about the Individual Education Plan (IEP)[11] in a school system. It may go by many other titles and names, but we all know what it means. It's supposed to be for and about the child; to be sure they have a good program for their needs. When we had Lisa, we were thrown into a new world. We learned a lot of new acronyms that stood for things that were perplexing to us. Here are just a few: IDEA:[12] Individuals with Disabilities Education Act, FAPE:[13] Free Appropriate Public Education, as well as LRE:[14] Least Restrictive Environment, IEE:[15] Independent Educational Evaluation, ESY: Extended School Year[16] and SPED which stands for Special Education.

We had no idea about all the different programs offered, all the different support people who would be involved in Lisa's life, and all the times we would have to fight for what we thought was right for Lisa. The educators seemed to have a different idea about what was best for Lisa, and in the beginning, we went along with what was suggested, as we were new to these procedures in the school system. But with each meeting, each new placement in a specific program in the school system, and each change, major or minor, I began to find my horns and dig in my heels and use my voice, for Lisa. My polite husband was quieter and kinder than I, and I sometimes came to a meeting with my radar up, feeling that they were trying to "pull a fast one" on us. I guess the differences between my husband and I were a good thing, for we balanced each other out at the IEP "discussion" table, and we each came up with great ideas that ultimately helped Lisa to be who she is today. At some point, I am sure the educators did not think well of us because we went from being mild mannered, compliant parents who didn't have a clue, to parents who stood their ground when we believed our vision for Lisa was good for Lisa, even though it might not be easy to achieve. There are many, many times that I could write about such things that have happened in Lisa's school years, but I will not bore you with most of them.

The following poem was written *after* we had a big meeting; a meeting to help get ready for Lisa's upcoming opportunity to attend her neighborhood school. What struck me about the meeting was the unbalanced representation at the IEP gathering. My husband and I walked into a fourth grade classroom and saw this huge group of people who all had something to do with Lisa's education, including the school principal, the regular and special educational classroom teachers who currently worked with Lisa, the regular and special educational teachers who would be working with her in the new school setting, speech, physical and occupational staff, the assistant director of the special educational program, any other teachers in the past who might have some input and maybe some other personnel like classroom aides, PE teachers, and others who the school wanted present at this meeting. The crowd stunned us, for it was just Lisa's Dad and I on one the side of the table and *all* of them on the other side. Planning for Lisa to attend her neighborhood school, in a regular classroom with just resource center help, was a big step for the school system, for us and most definitely for Lisa. I believe Lisa was one of the first of the students with Down syndrome in this school district to attend her neighborhood school and not just settle for the special education classroom that was across town. The intimidation was nerve-wracking for me. My husband was cool, calm and collected. We made it through the meeting, and as a result Lisa attended the neighborhood school, something that ultimately helped many students long after Lisa was gone from that elementary school. We did not start this change, but when we heard it was an option, we embraced it and did everything possible to have it be a good, rewarding and successful venture for Lisa. The poem just came to me after that meeting, and to my surprise, was readily accepted to be printed in a special education newsletter, with many agreeing with the concept. Enjoy.

The Parent's IEP Fantasy

I tremble as I wait for the meeting to begin,

My palms sweat, my heart pounds,

and I'm screaming from within.

I close my eyes, and try to calm

the fears that I have now,

And wonder if it could be changed,

but I really don't know how.

Imagine such a meeting,

away from all the school fuss,

Away from hard, miniature chairs

and tables that divides us.

Could it happen in our home,

with soft couches, chairs and lighting?

Some tea and cookies, if you please;

it may promote less fighting.

The educators could mingle
with the parents of the child,
And each could know the other
by visiting for a while.

Could those hundred dollar words they use
be said a simpler way,
So all could understand
what each person had to say?
No more intimidation
or poor tactics on either part,
Just simple, open-mindedness
and caring from the heart.

If by chance we disagree,
could the paper go unsigned?
Could we still work together;
leave our differences behind?
The child's basic welfare
should be our goal each day,
Not what will work for others
or just one person's say.
Then suddenly I awaken,
it is not what it has seemed.
None of this has happened;
it was only just a dream.

Having Friends

There are lots of songs and shows about friends. I have always believed friends are important, whether we are children or adults, so I made a conscious effort to encourage Lisa to make and keep friends. It's a lot of work, and looking at her track record, I don't think we did very well in the friends department. In grade school, it was fairly easy to get her involved with school activities, either during or after school. That would give her contact with others her age. With these peers, we would get Lisa to name someone who she liked, or with whom she might have done something on a one on one basis. The next step was to encourage Lisa to get a phone number from one of these contacts, so she could call to talk to them. This was difficult, because she was naturally shy, quiet and reserved. Once in awhile, she actually did talk to someone and got a phone number. The next step was even more difficult; getting her to call this friend to arrange an evening or a weekend activity.

There were several steps we had to go through before Lisa could actually secure a get-together. The first was to decide what they would like to do. In grade school, it would range from coming over to play, going out for a treat (either a movie or food) or choosing a physical activity such as roller-skating or swimming. Once Lisa decided what to do, we had to decide how to ask that person, planning each step from start to finish. We began with pretending to dial the number and saying "Hello, is (insert name of individual she was calling) there?" When that person got on the phone it continued with "Hi, this is Lisa Barcus." There was very little small talk. The next statement would be the reason for the call. "Would you like to (insert place to go) with me on (insert date and time)?"

Lisa and I had to decide all this ahead of time, and have her practice saying it several times. When she thought she was ready, we reached for the phone and did it for real! She would be nervous, which made her dialing skills rather shaky. But, finally she'd get the home of the special someone she was calling and begin her rehearsed speech. We ran into several snags, especially when the conversation didn't go according to practice. The first was when Lisa would ask for the friend, only to be told that the person wasn't at home. A look of panic in Lisa's face told me something was wrong. Lisa would just stand there with the phone up in the air, but away from her ear. Her shoulders were shrugged up near her ears, and her mouth was either open or turned to a frown.

She would be wide-eyed as was physically possible, without her eyes literally popping out. She might try to make a sound, but I could not understand any of her actual words. The next flaw in our well-practiced routine would be if she reached her friend, got through the asking process, then either that person didn't want to go or couldn't go with Lisa. Again, the drooped, bodily transformation and the unrecognizable sound from Lisa occurred immediately. That's when I would either say, "What! What's the matter?" or "Talk into the phone. Tell them…." I usually ended up taking the phone from her and talking to whoever was on the other line.

Even when she got through everything the entire process, the hello, the question and the confirmation of time and activity, I usually ended up with the phone anyway. This was to make sure Lisa got it all correct, or to talk to her friend's parent to verify the information.

She has come a long way since those early phone calls. I guess practice really does make perfect.

To practice making and keeping friends was a forever job, because each year brought changes, either in the school Lisa attended or because of the numerous new students who came and went. In the elementary levels, identifying her friends was a challenge. I didn't know all the kids in her class, so her system was to tell me a significant piece of information to identify the person. One of the best descriptions that Lisa came up with was when she would talk about Jenny "with the glasses." The name Jenny was popular and there was more than one Jenny that she knew, and several of those Jennies also wore glasses. As a result, I still didn't know for sure whom it was that Lisa was talking about. And if I had to pick Jenny with the glasses out of a crowd, I couldn't because odds were, most of the girls Lisa knew had glasses. The other friend was someone named Kenny. I hadn't heard his name often in Lisa's account of the day, but she would mention 'a boy' once in awhile. Lisa finally gave him a name with an adjective to help me (or was it to help Lisa) identify him better. Lisa referred to him as "Kenny with the haircut." My one question, if I dared to ask Lisa, would confuse her but I thought was funny. What is he called when his hair grows out?

Having friends, making friends and keeping friends is a natural process for most people. With Lisa it was an on-going quest. The best friends were in the elementary years. With the several moves we made, Lisa's attendance at different schools and less after school activities, it got more difficult for Lisa to maintain friends. The experiences she has had have helped her in other situations, so practice does help. It just must have been frustrating for her to always have to make new friends.

I kept telling myself that the friends kids made in their school years, especially the early years, may not be those same friends they would have after they had graduated from school. Granted, some of their high school friends could remain close for years to come, but it would probably be unusual to remain close for a lifetime. With Lisa, who has spent a lot of time in special services, resource classes or in some type of pullout sessions, she had little chance to form good solid friendships, let alone carry them with her to new states, towns and schools. So our moves have not been favorable for her to make long lasting friendships.

We finally settled in a town, and the friends are now more evident. I'm not sure they are all considered friends, but maybe more appropriately could be identified as acquaintances. I imagined Lisa having friends who would be there when she needed help, compassion and friendship. And these adult friends are. In her younger years, her circle of friends was made up of adults who worked with her in some way, a few students she had classes with, and the children in the neighborhood who knew her. Now, her friends include the group of people she goes out with to activities, including some staff personnel and other people with and without disabilities. She has learned how to approach people, get along with others, and join in activities that interest her. She seems happy, and content. I think her hard work has paid off. Just ask her friends.

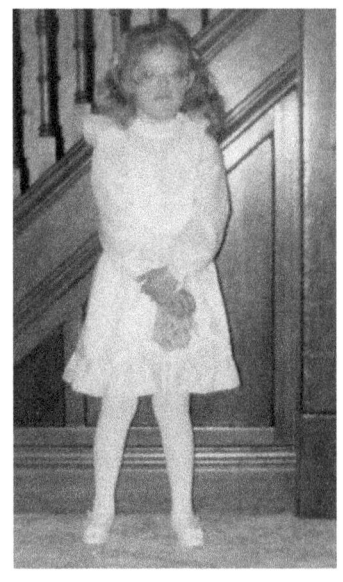

Letting Go Truly Difficult for Mom

How many times do I have to let go, to let Lisa grow and mature, to let her be independent of me? How do I loosen those apron strings and how many times does it take? I don't know the answers, but I do know I will always try to do the best for Lisa. If letting go will help her become an independent adult, that's what I'll do, but someone may have to pry my fingers loose from the tight hold I have on Lisa.

I got my first dose of relinquishment quite a few years ago. One of Lisa's special ed grade school teachers invited her and several other classmates to spend the night. They were to go home with the teacher on a Thursday night after school let out. They would go to her house, which was some 45 miles away, spend the night, and the teacher would bring them back to school on Friday. This particular year, there were three second-grader girls (it was a small class size) who were invited to spend the night and all three accepted. Lisa was one of them.

I didn't mention it to Lisa until the day before, for her sake…no, probably for mine. I think I wanted to have an easy out in case I changed my mind; then she would never know. When I finally told Lisa, she was so excited. She wanted to pick out her clothes and help pack right away. We managed to pick out one pair of PJs, toiletries and an extra set of clothes, which all fit in her school bag. If we had taken all that Lisa wanted, we would have needed a large travelers suitcase that pulls using a long handle and rolls on wheels.

Lisa's bedtime on Wednesday night was somewhat solemn for me. I knew she would not be there on Thursday night, so I was truly hesitant for Wednesday night to be done. Can you believe I purposely prolonged the book reading routine, prayers and last drink of water rituals to include two of each? Plus, I included some quiet sharing time with Lisa before she settled down to sleep!

Worse than bedtime though, was seeing her get on the bus in the morning, knowing I would not see her for some 32 hours; but who was counting! Off she went to enjoy a day of school with her teacher, to go home and spend the night with her teacher, and then be in school all day Friday with her teacher. Somehow, I thought maybe one of them might get tired of being with the other, though I didn't know who.

I can't tell you what went on with Lisa during all that time, except for the secondhand information the teacher shared. I wish I could have been in on the ride to her house, invisible and watching three usually talkative second-graders acting like silent little statues in the back seat of a strange car.

Pizza for supper, a favorite of all, must have helped because the teacher reported they ate lots and had fun visiting. I'm sure the bathtub routine was hectic, and this is one time I would not want to be there. Can you imagine a bath-giving assembly line? Get the first out and dressed, make sure the second used soap and try to amuse the third, who was waiting impatiently. No, thank you!

Bedtime at her house also included a book, but the teacher said she didn't make them read like she might do at school. Instead, she read to them and let them get snug, comfy and relaxed in their beds. It sounded like their evening was fun and busy. Mine was so different, I could hardly stand it. Right after work, my car seemed to be on automatic pilot toward the babysitter's house. I had to steer it all the way home. At home, I realized I did not have to know where Lisa was or what she was doing, but I sure wanted to know. Our family suppertime was quiet and quick. I could eat my own meal without having to get up for the forgotten things Lisa always asked for. I did try, jokingly, to cut my husband's meat, but he reassured me he'd be careful with the knife and that he was able to cut the meat by himself. The evening went by ever so slowly, though I did enjoy sitting down and taking some personal time to read a book without interruptions. Without Lisa there, I could do anything I wanted. I just didn't know what I wanted to do with all that spare time I had.

Finally, the day was done, and by morning things should have been better. But for me, they were not. A sad sort of emptiness was noticeable, even though my husband and the other three children were there. There was the same sort of fumbling with a lot of time on my hands, and the same loneliness. Soon my workday was over, and it was time to get Lisa. It took her awhile to talk about her sleep over, but by evening it was no-stop talking about all that had happened.

The teacher's note also helped me to fill in some blank areas Lisa seemed to forget to share. All in all, it sounded like a successful adventure for those three second-graders and one brave teacher. I am glad I let her go. It helped me to stand back and see how life is, and could be with and without Lisa. I'll take life with Lisa anytime! She fills my day, my heart and my life.

Girl Scouts

The Girl Scout mission: Girl Scouting builds girls of courage, confidence and character, who make the world a better place. And further in the information we received about Girl Scouting it said "Through activities… Girl scouting provides girls with opportunities for fun and friendship while fostering the development of leadership skills and self-esteem."

This is what I wanted for Lisa. With some planning, we had her join a Girl Scout troop. After some discussion with teachers and Girl Scout leaders, it was decided a neighborhood group would be better than one in her school she currently attended, which was across town from where we live. There would be a better chance of seeing her friends and having them over to visit if she joined the neighborhood troop.

Her first visit was towards the end of the school year, when projects were completed and no new ones were started. She was able to join in with singing, playing simple games and a music activity. She fit in well; the girls welcomed her, befriended her and helped her when she needed it. She was ready to join the Girl Scout troop on a regular basis.

After Lisa's first visit, according to the troop leader, the Girl Scouts were going to meet on Mondays after school. I was all set on Monday morning to get her there. I made sure Lisa had her Brownie dress on, with the cute little orange tie at the collar, and the sash draped on her right shoulder. Her white crew socks along with her black and white saddle shoes completed the outfit. I made sure her sitter knew of this very special first meeting. Lisa would not be dropped off at the sitter's after school as we usually did. I also made sure the bus driver knew where to take Lisa, what side of the school to drop her off and who would be there to help her. I made sure that Lisa's older brother had a note to take to the teacher, requesting he leave his classroom early, in order to be ready and waiting when Lisa arrived at that school. I made sure I was able to get off work in time to pick her up at the school after the meeting. What happened?

There was no meeting. They had met the Monday before and only got together every other week. Oops, my mistake. And guess what I did the next week? I forgot to dress her, forgot to let anyone know it was a Girl Scout day, just simply, I forgot. And the next week she was sick, and the next week, I tried to send her after it ended for the year. And so it went. As it turns out, she was only at one meeting for this first try at attending Girl Scouts. During the summer, the Girl Scouts only met once or twice, and the leader assured me Lisa would be invited, but that didn't happen. When fall came around, Lisa finally got to go to another meeting, and afterwards brought home information about her being sworn in as a member of the Brownie troop at the next meeting. I took off work early to attend this special rite of passage and arrived there early enough to find a seat close to the circle.

I looked around at the group of girls and finally found Lisa, standing very still near a small table. I sat more upright in my chair, my heart speeding up some; a little nervous, I guess. I told myself to take another breath. Whew, that was better. While waiting for her turn, Lisa wiggled at her place in line. She bent down to touch her toes, pulled up her tights, and straightened her sash. The white tablecloth was wrinkled; she straightened it out. While she leaned on the table, propped up by her left elbow, her name was called.

Thank you Mrs. Girl Scout leader, for making this ritual look normal and rehearsed. "Lisa, repeat after me. On my honor…" Silence. Then slowly, and ever so quietly, she begins, "On my honor…" Now why were my eyes glistening, why couldn't I blink the tears away? With her hand raised, three fingers up, the Girl Scout sign, she completed the pledge, accepted a pin and sat down, just like the others had done. If she never did any more with the Girl Scouts, that in itself was well worth it. Thank you, Mrs. Girl Scout leader, for working with her, for accepting her, for allowing her to realize this dream of hers. Thank you for following the Girl Scout slogan: Do a good turn daily. You will never know how much this meant to me and to Lisa. Thank you.

Mastering Math

Before there is math, there is counting. Learning to count is a matter of repetition, and repetition means over and over and over. Thank goodness for the fun and entertaining children's shows that did this with music, poems, rhymes and never-ending repetition. One poem I grew up with is still around and kids continue to recite it to this day. I'm sure you remember "One, two, buckle my shoe…"

When Lisa was learning to count, we counted everything; even when she couldn't pronounce the words distinctly. We counted bites of cereal, blocks and toys, walking up and down steps, how many times we could let the phone ring, buttons on shirts, eyes, ears, nose and fingers and toes. Any chosen object that could be counted was counted, which meant we counted just about everything.

Starting with something concrete helped Lisa when we introduced the visual number. It's one thing to count items out loud, but to say that the word "one" has a written symbol, 1, and it is *this* many blocks, could be confusing. It was also at this time that one block would be presented to show it as a tangible item. Talking about "one" and seeing "one," then having that concept be understood took awhile for Lisa. We kept at it, over and over again, just like the counting. This meant I needed to stretch my patience, while waiting for her to count, say ten blocks. It took all my will power to sit quietly while she counted ever so slowly, with a questioning tone behind every number said, clearly unsure if it was the correct sequence. From there she started to do some addition, a new form of trial and error. How hard is it to realize that $1 + 1 = 2$? On paper, it was difficult in the beginning, but with the help of blocks and marshmallows and other objects, she got the idea. I believe the marshmallows and cereal worked the best, because as an incentive for her to give correct answers, she got to eat the "sum." There was a point when we had to do away with the food rewards or Lisa would have become overweight at a very early age.

From a young age, tactile learning was more successful with Lisa and teachers discovered that early on. From counting and simple math problems, Lisa moved on to knowing time and money. I think these skills will always be useful because understanding time and money are utilized daily.

There were times when we would practice money skills or clock times over and over, and finally she just couldn't take it anymore. When this happened, you would know it right away, because she would just shut down. And when that happened, there was no changing her, no reasoning with her and no hope for a break in the silence. She could hold out longer than anyone and if someone tried to have a power struggle, they may not like the outcome. One of her elementary teachers learned the hard way.

This teacher was a substitute in the classroom on occasion and didn't know Lisa very well. We had learned over those first few years that if Lisa began to shut down on a task, refusing to work or engage in a conversation, that was a clue to change directions. It would be as easy as having the teacher change her tactics, from a question/answer format to multiple choice or some other method. The trick was to switch gears so Lisa would think we had quit that approach, yet still get the work done. Sometimes that meant changing from her writing the answers on paper to writing on the board, or giving verbal answers, or using textures to arrive at the same result, the answer. It worked most of the time, for those who knew Lisa. The substitute teacher didn't have a clue, and didn't seem to want to do it any other way than her "teacher" way. Bad mistake for that substitute. The initial incident probably dealt with a math problem in some way, which was Lisa's least favorite subject. Lisa shut down after many frustrating tries, not to be won over by the substitute who continued to teach the math session. Lisa would not talk, let alone work and the more the substitute would insist on it, the more stubborn Lisa was. The notebook had entries on her not cooperating, and other adults in the room related some facts that made my "mother instinct to protect" kick in. Sometimes, according to other adults in the classroom, Lisa would cry. That was not necessary, and I was not about to let Lisa suffer through this substitute teacher's power struggle without help. I also didn't want Lisa to hate learning, and if she ended up crying while trying to learn, it just didn't seem the right way to do things.

Because Lisa's regular teacher was unavailable due to an illness, this substitute teacher actually sat in on an IEP (Individual Educational Plan) just a day after a major power struggle incident and afterwards, she probably wished she'd never taught Lisa. I don't believe she read Lisa's IEP, because there were things she wasn't aware of and didn't do, according to what had been written in the current IEP. As it happened, the substitute teacher brought up some concerns or problems she was having with Lisa, and was suggesting other things that my husband and I thought were inappropriate for any teaching technique. We dealt with this substitute teacher, discussed what she had proposed, and ended the IEP by walking out without signing it. The normal routine was to sign the IEP after we updated the plans, which would verify that we agreed with the changes. We didn't this time. This didn't happen very often with us, as we were usually pretty agreeable back then. I'm sure that substitute truly didn't understand the parent point of view, and I sure didn't understand the reasons for her tactics or the pre-written IEP changes she came up with. We ended on a real unhappy note. Next, I called an assistant director of the special education program to give him our side of the story. What was simply a situation the substitute teacher could have easily solved by changing her techniques, turned in to an awkward circumstance for all of us. I told the assistant director in no uncertain terms, that I would *never* allow Lisa to have that person as a teacher again. That meant as a substitute or in any other capacity.

I am sure this caused some fill-in problems when it came to staffing in Lisa's classroom, but I do know that Lisa never had that individual teacher in her classroom again, throughout all her years at this specific school district. That may seem a bit harsh, but the reason at stake was Lisa and her education. There were certain ways Lisa learned best, and those were to be utilized to give her the best possible chance in the real world. We had decided this in IEP meetings when Lisa first entered the school system, and it was written in the IEP. All that needed to be done was for the person who would be teaching Lisa to read her IEP, understand and follow the IEP.

Lisa did learn; she mastered counting, numbers, simple math, time, reading writing, and many other cognitive skills. She learned in the way that worked best for her, and for the most part, from teachers who realized her potential. I applaud the teachers who looked past her congenital diagnosis of Down syndrome, which included both intellectual and developmental disability issues, to see that there was the possibility for Lisa to learn, and they helped her be the best she could be. There were some rough patches along the way, but together, the end result was successful. Lisa spent most of her educational years in regular educational programs, with support from special education teachers. She graduated with her class, and went out into the work force as a contributing, tax-paying citizen. This is what it's all about. This is what we envisioned.

The Neighborhood School

Lisa had always wanted to go to our neighborhood school where her brothers and sister went. Then one day, her wish came true. Preparations ahead of time by teachers and staff made the transition smooth and easy for Lisa. The first step was for Lisa to spend a few days at the school and in the classroom that would soon become her classroom. Her "soon-to-be" classmates were involved in informational sessions about Lisa. This had a neat effect in our neighborhood. Several young girls came over to our house on different days to visit Lisa. They introduced themselves as classmates who were anxiously awaiting her visit in the coming week. They were considerate, courteous and most of all, full of questions. By being with her several times before her visit, they learned more about her and she looked forward to seeing her friends at school. She now had friends in the neighborhood that recognized her as a person, called her by name and encouraged her participation in activities with them.

Lisa chose to walk to the neighborhood school on that first visiting day, something she never had a choice about before. One of her older brothers walked with her, and with each block they were greeted and joined by others in the neighborhood. Lisa was going to the neighborhood school, and they were just as excited as she was.

I would love to have been in that school building for those first three days to watch what went on. I only know what Lisa, her brother and the teachers related to me. Rumor has it she visited the school nurse three times in less than two hours. I figured it probably did happen, because Lisa knew the nurse, who was a familiar and friendly face to Lisa, and Lisa was able to sweet talk the teacher into letting her go. Lisa is good at doing that. Lisa had a buddy for practically every class she was in; some appointed, some volunteered. She said she enjoyed the different classes and the children, and that she made lots of friends. One must have been extra special to Lisa because her first evening at home after school Lisa insisted on making a special present for this new friend. Lisa spent a lot of time deciding what to give her. Later, Lisa wrapped it and wrote a nice note to her. Some of it was in code, I think, as I was unable to decipher all of the words.

Lisa's new friends showed her the layout of the school, where the bathroom was, what to do with her coat and most importantly, how to get to the Resource Room. Lisa had been attending a Resource Room at her other school for some time so that was not new. The newness was all the help and attention she received. I really can't blame the other children though, because Lisa was unique and different, and all them wanted a chance to be with her. They really went out of their way at lunch, or so I heard. One young girl was so helpful that she was feeding Lisa her lunch. But worse than that, Lisa let her! Lisa always tried to get out of doing everything, so this shouldn't have surprised me.

Naturally, my worst fear was that Lisa would be teased, stared at or made to feel out of place. If there was any of this going on, it was not in front of Lisa. I could tell she felt welcomed and comfortable there because she would tell me how her day was and it was always on a positive and upbeat note. Her classmates would become her friends. It looked like this was the right option for Lisa. On the final day of her *visit* week at our neighborhood school, Lisa hesitated when it was time to leave. She would like to have stayed at that time, and when I would ask her about it later, she said she wanted to go back. My fondest memory of those three days was an event that happened on her last morning. I had taken Lisa and her brother to school, wanting to be involved in whatever way I could. As Lisa was getting out of the car, she saw one of her new friends, and called her by name. This young girl turned around to see Lisa and hear her shout, "Wait up!" I sat there and watched the two of them chatting for a minute and then turn towards the school entrance. They walked into school together, as any two friends would do.

Halloween is a Treat

Every year, I was always surprised by how quickly Halloween came around. I was convinced that the calendar was incorrect, as I was sure that we still had some leftover candy from last year. The container I hid on the top shelf behind the crock-pot was usually half full of stale Tootsie Rolls and old, sticky suckers. This was the confiscated candy, taken away when I noticed my kids bouncing off the walls after they collected all their trick-or-treat candy. And yet they always wanted to use a grocery bag for their anticipated heaps of treats each year.

Isn't it funny how every year as the child gets older, the sack gets bigger? Lisa went from a sandwich bag to lunch sack size bag, and I just hoped she would never get greedy enough to want a grocery sack. We have always taught our children it is better to give than to receive, but try telling that to a young trick-or-treater. Lisa also tried to refined the technique, unlike her older brothers who traveled at light speed, door to door, in a contest to see who could fill their sacks first.

Lisa was eighteen months old when she experienced trick or treating for the first time. She could not yet walk, so we carried her down the sidewalk on one side of the street. This was plenty for her and us. The next year, she had only been walking confidently for only a few months. Our mistake was that we did not have her practice walking outside. After she tripped several times because of uneven sidewalks, we carried her again. The third year, she walked (thank goodness) the entire distance of a double block. I am sure she went this distance because she was inspired by the finer methods she learned about Halloween while in preschool. Teachers and their students learned a variety of ways to address the act of asking for Halloween treats.

The students practiced trick-or-treating throughout the month of October, usually by having one of the adults *hide* in the bathroom. I think that was the only door they could open and shut a lot. If they used the classroom door that opened into the hallway, I imagine several of the students would have taken the opportunity to go exploring while the others were learning proper trick or treat etiquette.

The first young volunteer would go timidly to the bathroom door that was shut, and begin the routine while the other classmates watched intensely. First, was the sound of a rapid knock from inside the bathroom. This was a clue for the scared student to begin. This was loud and harsh, and it always took Lisa by surprise, startling her and making her act very timid. Now it was up to the student to knock on the door as if they were at a house for trick or treating. After waiting to see if the student would make the appropriate move, which they seldom did, a helpful adult would open the door and pretend to greet the spooky goblin.

The adult in the bathroom usually knelt on the tile floor, moaning something about being too old for this kind of activity. The class always anticipated what was to happen next, and instead of letting the adult give the clue for those magic words, they quickly resounded "Trick or Treat!" I was always confused as to who got tricked and who got treated. Lisa seemed to be puzzled as well. She would stand by the doorway of the bathroom and nervously sway back and forth with her head down. It looked as if she had just noticed her shoes for the very first time. Lisa would whisper something about not getting any candy from the adult, and could she go to the bathroom, please.

On Lisa's first real walking year to trick-or-treat in the neighborhood, she would simply hold out her bag, smile innocently and just say "Please." You can also be assured she answered the sound of a plunk of candy in her sack with a nice, but quiet "Thank you." The next year, she learned to say trick or treat, though it was barely audible and somewhat hard to understand when she pronounced it as one word. As she got older, she would probably like to have just said, "Give me the candy," because she learned to go a little faster and a little further. But she still maintained proper trick or treat etiquette.

We have had a lot of years celebrating Halloween, and the entire family still likes to make this a big event. I myself have dressed up a little for the occasion, even though the kids insisted a mask wasn't necessary for me. Our supper was always quick and easy, with very little eaten in anticipation of all that sweet, yummy candy.

The kids dressed in their costumes way too early, and then stood around waiting for dusk and the witching hour. I say stood, because sitting in those store-bought, plastic outfits was almost impossible. The costumes would rip out under the arms or legs, and it was nearly impossible to sew the plastic. Staples and tape are not much better for plastic repairs either, though I have tried all those techniques. When Lisa went out on Halloween, she would start with a clean costume and smudge-free eyeglasses. When she arrived back at home, the outfit looked like a taste-testing station down the front of her, and if it was the least bit cool outside, her glasses were steamed and smeared. This made it difficult for her to see what was in the bag of goodies. Of course, at the end of the walk, I could not tell what had been in her sack except by examining all the empty candy bar wrappers. It was also a given that she'd been eating the candy because I could see it on her face, nose, chin and sometimes her hair. Definitely a bath night.

Lisa would come home with tired legs, a stomach full of candy and her outfit in pieces. She would now be satisfied to drink some nice warm apple cider and help give out treats. She enjoyed this too, but people would sure look at her funny when they would knock on our door, I would open it, and Lisa hollered "TRICK OR TREAT!"

Food Choices

There is something about Thanksgiving that makes people think of eating. It must be all that food; the turkey, stuffing, mashed potatoes and gravy, pies and whatever else people choose for this special holiday. Our family managed to over indulge on this huge spread of food, and loved the fact that there would be leftovers.

I have always watched Lisa's eating habits, encouraging a balanced diet with only an occasional splurge. An individual who has Down syndrome needs to be concerned with food consumption because there is a tendency to be overweight. Lisa has always liked to eat, but was never really obsessed until one summer when she was about seven years old.

She was sick with an undiagnosed siege of flu-like symptoms and unable to eat much of anything. She had a hospital stay, but no conclusive results from the many tests that were done When she began to feel better, she acted like she was trying to make up for lost time. I remember on incident when her taste in foods did not agree with mine. The worst account was when she viewed a dog food commercial and said, "That looks good!"

Her favorite snack was, is and probably always will be peanut butter with crackers. When she was younger, she asked for peanut butter with crackers on it. That made me wonder if she wanted the peanut butter spread on the palm of her hand, topped with a cracker. I never tried it with her, but encouraged her to think about what she was saying and to ask for a cracker with peanut butter on it. A saltine cracker is her first choice, but in a pinch graham cracker will do. For an added treat, if I had any on hand, she would spread chocolate chip canned frosting over the peanut butter and cracker. This is m-m-m-m good, really! Lisa would ask for this snack anytime, sometimes for breakfast with some fruit or eggs, or for lunch, instead of peanut butter on bread. Her favorite time to eat this snack was after school, before supper and as a bedtime snack. Yes, you're getting the idea; she could eat this snack all the time. It was good, somewhat nutritious (the peanut butter anyway) and easy to make, so I really didn't worry. As she got older and more capable, she would even make her own, which helped me sometimes, even though cleanup time took twice as long.

Another of Lisa's favorite foods was and still is mashed potatoes. She had this a lot when she was in the hospital. They must have had a mashed potato machine similar to those ice cream machines at restaurants. It seemed easy enough for them to bring in her favorite order, mashed potatoes with gravy, any time of the day or night. After being in the hospital two days and not eating, the mashed potatoes finally did the trick to get her to start to eat again. She had seconds and thirds, as I recall. She had mashed potatoes for breakfast as well. And she loved to change her menu plan to include mashed potatoes if it was not among the choices. I thought, "This is great, she's eating again, and starting to feel better."

I almost changed my mind one very early morning when she was still in the hospital. Lisa said she was hungry and nothing I could say would change her mind. I tried to tell her that 4:00 a.m. was not the time to be eating and that she could wait until breakfast for her special order. She continued to insist on calling the nurse, and I finally gave in. Besides, I was confident the nurse could handle this situation. I knew the outcome would be in my favor, which meant we could go back to sleep. That didn't happen.

Lisa pushed the nurse button that was answered quickly. Lisa politely asked for mashed potatoes and gravy. The nurse did not even bat an eyelash. Her response to Lisa was that she would call the order in immediately, and would bring the food as soon as it was ready. As the nurse walked out, Lisa turned to me and smugly said "*See!*" So there I sat, at four in the morning, in a dimly lit hospital room with my PJs on, reading a book and occasionally looking up to see Lisa enjoying one of her favorite foods.

Although she was careful of how much she ate, she has not been able manage her diet enough to avoid the fact of being overweight. At Thanksgiving, as with any special event, Lisa will want to eat all her favorite foods. Now that she's on her own, I can't monitor the portions and number of helpings, but will remind her about good choices. Hopefully, in doing this, we can maintain a proper weight for her, fuel her body with the right foods and still satisfy her taste buds.

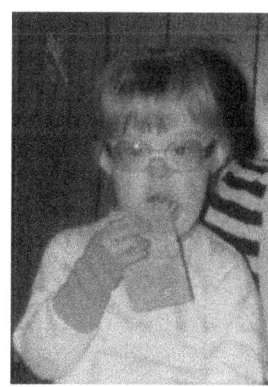

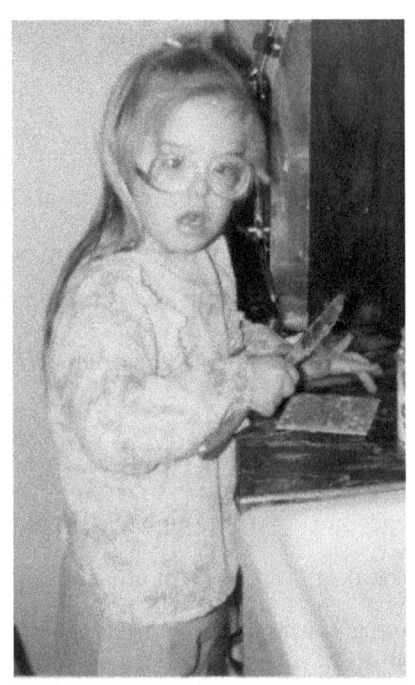

First Communion

One of the proudest moments for me was when, at the age of eight, Lisa made her First Communion. I thought I would have to do some fast-talking to get Lisa enrolled in the afternoon classes, but was pleasantly surprised when our church readily accepted her. Her first after school class was tension-filled for me. I was concerned with her getting along with others, and if she would actively participate. The teachers put my mind to rest, reassured me afterwards by stating how well she did, answered some of my questions, and all in all said Lisa was good.

There was a special program of enrollment at church, which Lisa also attended. All the children were asked to walk up to the front of church and sign a special book. I explained this to Lisa, who listened intently. I also said that they would call her name, which would be her cue to know when to walk up. As we sat patiently waiting, there were names being called and children walking up. Lisa started to squirm and really became agitated. She finally blurted out "That's not fair. When is it my turn?" Soon it was. She heard her name, and smartly marched up to the book that was placed the table. The priest handed her a pen, and we all watched silently. After she painstakingly wrote LISA, she stopped and put her pen down. The priest bent down and asked if she could also write her last name. Lisa answered very loudly and proudly "SURE," then promptly and painstakingly slow, wrote her last name. I was so elated, for I knew how long she has been practicing to first write legibly, and to remember the letters of her last name. No one else in that church could have known how I felt at that moment.

It seemed as Lisa got older, I became a little more defensive, or maybe just more in tune to people and their judgments about Lisa. I had first recognized this the day the children signed the first communicants' book. I thought the sermon on that first Sunday of Lent was kind of unusual, bearing in mind that Lisa was one of those who signed the book that day. The priest talked about the Lenten season, and I heard him say this will be an up season, not a down season. Here I was, with Lisa, and I also saw another child with Down syndrome in the next row, and the priest is talking *up* season. The priest, in his sermon, aptly designated that Lenten season as the UP season, when Lisa, who has Down syndrome, would make her First Communion. Is that a coincidence or what? Do you see what I'm getting at? It really hit me funny, in a good sort of way. And last but not least, ironically, on the day of her First Communion, the Knights of Columbus held their annual tootsie roll drive that helps the individuals who have a developmental disability. Coincidence again, I'm sure, but a very interesting one at that. I am probably the only one to see these oddities, to know that it really doesn't need to make sense. All I know is that Lisa very proudly and reverently walked up for her First Communion, not knowing the impact she had on the family or me. She was just doing the appropriate and natural thing. And I was very proud of her for that.

School Pictures: Preserving Memories

There is something quirky about those school pictures. You know the ones; the billfold size, elementary student pictures of a cute boy or girl, with hair combed, face washed, teeth brushed and an invisible but suggestive halo above their head. We, as parents, see to it that our child's picture is the best. It all starts way back, when the parent took that first picture in the hospital. Remember unwrapping your newborn baby, counting all the fingers and toes, marveling at this miracle of God and saving the moment forever by taking a picture of your precious one.

I remember seeing Lisa through my tears as I looked intently for the obvious signs of Down syndrome, all the while giving some excuse for each sign that I would see. In those pictures at birth, she had no neck, a little fuzz-top head and eyes that looked just fine to me, no matter what angle or slant they took on. At the age of three months, she still had no neck, a little more fuzz and eyes that definitely gave her that unique syndrome look. I tried to convince myself that she did not have Down syndrome, and I was sure Lisa was the cutest baby ever, except for my other three babies, who were also very cute. Naturally.

Those first pictures of Lisa are of her lying on my hospital bed, garbed in a pajama sack with long sleeves and no place for her hands to go. The hands are covered to discourage hand or thumb sucking, as well as keeping them warm. My ignorant thought was, "Don't they know she has Down syndrome, and probably will never be able to get her hand to her mouth!" Little did I know that I should never say "never."

Looking at those pictures now, I still get teary-eyed, but they are happy tears, remembering the good times, knowing and loving her, and looking to the future and all she *could* do. Every three months during Lisa's first year of life was professional picture-taking time because a child's features can change quickly in a year's time, and that's how often I had pictures taken of my other children, every three months.

But with Lisa, her changes were very subtle. At three months, she had control over her head, but not enough to stay upright without propping. At six months old, head control was better, but the sitting was still wobbly. I remember all the times the discount store offered photos, and I would patiently wait for that perfect smile, and quickly move away for that perfect snap of the picture. I made sure I always caught her before she tumbled over. It's a big drop from the white, fake bearskin covering the table to the hard, painted cement floor.

It was also difficult to draw her attention to the camera, especially when the backdrop was closer and more colorful. I hope people don't remember me as the mother who would act a little wild and crazy just to get her daughter's attention. Of course, the cameraperson also looked pretty silly, making "goo-goo" noises and playing with the different toys that should have enticed Lisa, but really didn't.

From six months to nine months, to one year to two years, Lisa's pictures were all about the same. I can only tell Lisa's age by the change in backdrops or the length of her hair. A noticeable difference came when glasses were added. It made Lisa look more mature and classy and I could tell from the different style frames what year the picture was taken. One of my favorite pictures shows Lisa with her head bent slightly forward, looking over the top rim of her glasses, trying hard to see. And when her glasses were too far down on her nose, she looked like a little old Grannie.

Once Lisa reached grade school, we were in the big times with school pictures. Notes were sent home the week before, making sure the pictures were paid for in advance. One disadvantage for us parents was we no longer had the option to pick and choose the best pose. It's "take what you get," which means sometimes you have to ignore the one pigtail that is up higher than the other, or the barrette that is beginning to fall out. You can sometimes tell what Lisa had for breakfast, if her face wasn't washed well, or you can see the sore nose and chapped lips from a recent cold. Whatever the imperfections, I would never expect the teacher to have her looking perfect. They would have to do the same for each child, and I know that's next to impossible. That was the way Lisa always looked. Why not capture her true self? Sure. If I believed that, then why did I dress her up, curl her hair and send her to school looking more polished than she'd ever been. It's no wonder I didn't recognize that pretty face smiling back at me. Where's the dirt?

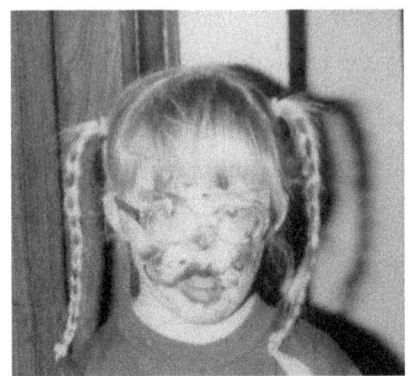

Lisa and Roller-skating

Lisa had mastered roller-skating while in elementary school but there was a time when she had a problem with skating. The problem was not in getting her there. She loved to go and always talked about who would be there and whom she would skate with. The problem was not getting the right skates or putting them on. She knew her size, how to lace them tightly and she even remembered to have two wheels tightened for easier skating. Having all those wheels turning 'round and 'round while she was trying to stand still was just too difficult for her if all four wheels were loose.

The problem was not in standing or moving on the carpet. She could handle both, if done at her pace and style, which meant little shuffle-shuffle steps and both feet in constant contact with the floor. The problem occurred once she reached that highly glossed wooden floor, if she ever did. She avoided the rink as long as she could, first visiting the video games, concession stand and the bathroom. All those places she could get to by being on the carpet. After she used all her excuses, and received lots of encouragement from me, she would head for the monstrous floor. This was when the outside wall came in handy. She would hold onto the wall from her first step out, and through her entire trip around the rink.

She moved very timidly, still trying to keep both feet in contact with the floor. When she moved too fast and lunged forward, her sudden, startled movements caused one foot to come up, and quickly down with a clunk. This caused her to grab the wall with two hands, while she tried desperately to hug it or find a good, stable handhold. There she would pause for a moment, resting I think.

Slowly, she looked around and found a friendly, familiar face, usually mine. She would give me a big, toothy smile, a thumbs up sign and hollered something like "I did it!" I would smile back, using one of my motherly smiles just for this type of situation, and think, "That's great, but I think you still have a long way to go to get completely around the rink." Things went along fairly well, with Lisa sometimes using only one hand on the wall or even braver, no hands. She remained close to the wall, but moved cautiously along using stiff, toy soldier-like leg movements.

Another problem arose when a person would whiz by a little too close, and the slight breeze seemed to knock her down. It was "kerplunk," flat on her bottom, legs up in the air and arms behind her in an effort to break her fall. As often as this happened, it's a small wonder she didn't break something. Her bloodcurdling scream led you to believe she had indeed broken at least one bone.

Following a fall, I would take a complete inventory of all her bones, a thorough inspection for any cuts and bruises, while quickly trying to convince her to finish going around the entire rink. Usually, a hard fall meant a definite concession stand exit. If she were a real trooper, she would finish but definitely had at least one hand on the wall again. She got pretty pokey at times and caused pileups of other youngsters just learning to skate. At times, a brave skater would try to pass Lisa, which really complicated matters.

Lisa would not move away from the wall, probably thinking "If that person wants to pass, let him go around me, away from the wall." Lisa would get helpful and lend a hand to the passerby, but there was trouble if the other person held on too tight.

Lisa would holler loudly while she tried to get her hand released from the other person's tight hold. Down they would go, with hurt feelings more than anything. If this helping hand option wasn't used, Lisa chose to just flatten herself up against the wall to make way for others who wanted to pass. She would be facing the wall, with her arms up high, palms flat and head turned toward the individual trying to pass. Her feet would still be pointed in the direction she was headed before she tried to move out of the way. It looked like she was in a half-twist position and frozen there. All her *skating* activity took place in the time span of one to one and a half hours. As she neared the exit to get off the rink, she would pick up speed, being enticed by the sights and sounds of the concession stand. That could be a little tricky, for right in front of the candy display was a patch of linoleum. A little slip sliding was always expected and she seemed to tolerate the possibility of a fall without complaints. It must have been worth it to get that special treat she thought was so well earned.

Winning, Spelling and Soda Caps

Lisa spent several minutes in front of the grocery store cooler, trying to decide which bottle of soda to pick. It had to have one of those winning caps where you could win a 1992 vehicle, (that was the newest car to buy at that time) a week at a hot vacation spot or a free pop. Nothing could rush this selection process. I waited patiently, and thought back to her changing attitudes on winning.

When Lisa first toddled around, she would want to run with her brothers, but her running wasn't any faster than when she walked. You could see a difference in her gait, only because she would lean her head and neck a little more forward, and her arms, with bent elbows and clenched fists, would move twice as fast. But she didn't actually move any faster; it just looked like it. If she was really into running that day, she would even huff and puff, leading you to believe that she was indeed at top speed. The end result was, if she walked the same distance, she would arrive at the same time.

Lisa did not and still doesn't like to have a foot race with anyone who can beat her. When she was younger, her brothers would get her to "run" just to encourage some exercise. If they made it competitive, and possibly moved ahead of her towards the finish line, she would immediately stop dead in her tracks, stomp her feet and holler, "No fair." I tried to explain to her that she couldn't always win, and that she'd never win if she quit running. It took some talking, but Lisa finally did make an effort to finish those friendly foot races, even though she would just as soon avoid anything that strenuous and competitive. (The concept of never quitting did stick with her, as is evident in some of her later challenges in life.)

I think the PE instructor at school had to have a lot of patience to keep Lisa on task and be willing to try some of the gym or outdoor activities they did. With Lisa's quarterly report card, we received an update of specific activities that she should have completed during PE time. She had to jump rope, hang from a bar, run a certain distance and throw or bounce a ball, among other things.

Lisa's sheet was not filled in with how many repetitions she had done, but rather, it showed that she attempted the activity and to what degree she was successful. She may not have been able to jump rope by herself, but she was working on becoming the best end-rope twirler there was. She may not have been able to hang from a bar, though I'd wonder if it might help stretch her a little to give her some height. And with running or doing ball activities, I didn't expect her to be the next volleyball star, but I was very proud of her when classmates remarked on how well she served the volleyball.

I have always known that she was not very active physically and that's okay. But give her spelling words on her level, plus a week to work on them, and she could come up with a fairly high score. Sometimes even 100 percent! The words got more difficult every year, and I was amazed at what she could accomplish academically, especially when there is a reward for that perfect paper. If I told Lisa that she could have a soda pop for a grade of 100 percent, I'd better be ready with the 60 cents after school.

The funny thing is, when she was at home writing me a note, the words were never spelled exactly right. It took me awhile to realize "caniviztheliberie" was not one word in a foreign language, but actually a request for her to "visit the library." She tried to communicate through writing and enjoyed leaving notes for me. She also didn't mind when I sat down with her to correct the spelling and told her about spacing to separate each word for easier reading. I sometimes even had her rewrite a note to see if she could do better the second time.

Her note writing and spelling words were good ways to encourage reading and writing, and hopefully it also continued to increase her abilities in this area. This also gave her a sense of accomplishment and probably built up her self-confidence. After each time that she aced a spelling test, she would strut around with her head held high, conveying an "I can do anything" attitude.

And now, back to the soda bottle cap. She finally chose a bottle of soda that she was certain would be a winner. She carried it carefully to the car, stopping occasionally to hold the bottle up high and try to look under the cap without taking it off. Lisa did this each time she chose a soda. When the cap was finally twisted off, she would look at it and read it. After that she would hand it to me to confirm the awful message. Yup, it said "Sorry, try again."

The first time the message was different, she looked at the cap, and instantly yelled "I won!" Of course, I thought of the new vehicle or vacation trip, only to be disappointed with her win of a free bottle of soda. But Lisa was so excited that she could hardly sit still. The next question from her, as she sat drinking that soda, was how soon could she use her winning cap to get a soda?

BARCUS

Size and Ability

Lisa's physical and mental abilities have always increased in varying stages and never at the same time. If she took off on a big growth spurt, mastering some gross motor skill like rolling over, sitting or walking, her fine motor abilities or mental gains would be put on hold. She would then excel in something like saying some new words, writing new letters or learning how to snap or button, and subsequently her gross motor skills would lag. Some of her skills were very impressive for her age or size, while at other times people wondered about her abilities for that same reason, her age or size.

It started on the day she was born, when she weighed in at 8 pounds, 13 ounces. According to the doctor, that was a higher birth weight than average for a newborn with Down syndrome. Right off the bat, she wasn't average. In comparison to my other children's birth weights, she was average. One child had a birth weight of 9 pounds 8 ounces, and the other two right around 8 pounds. But from the first day of her life, we have had to explain her age and abilities to others.

When she started talking before she was walking, people couldn't believe how clear and distinctive her verbal skills were. It was funny to have her saying two and three words at a time, yet we would have to carry her everywhere. But even after she started walking, the situation was still unusual. She was so petite and so short, that people thought she was too young to be walking. Someone who is two feet tall does look funny walking, but she got even more looks when I said she was over two years old and had just started walking.

Her height has not been a plus for her either. She sat in a car seat a lot longer than the other children, and it did not give her a very interesting view of the outdoors. All she saw was the solid part of the door, where the armrest and door handle were situated. She would strain her neck to look outside, and if she was lucky, she could probably see the trees and clouds. Not too exciting there either.

As she got older, she didn't get much taller, and things didn't get much better. The rides at the local and state fairs were very disappointing for her. She matured past the little kiddie rides, but didn't really outgrow them height-wise for a lot of years. The fast and scary rides were the rides she wanted to try, but her height kept her off for quite awhile. That was the down side, excuse the term, for her. I had no problem with her waiting to ride these faster attractions, so it worked out fine for me. There was an up side to her smaller physique. The obvious was in buying clothes for her. She could wear a pair of pants for several years. At first, she needed more waist than length, to allow for diaper room. Whatever fit around the waist, she wore. We rolled up the pant legs, or if others had worn them a lot before they got to Lisa, I even got creative enough to cut off the excess material at the bottom and sew a nice hem. It was better not to cut them, because once she got rid of the diapers, she was able to wear the pants for a longer period of time. In deciding whether to cut or roll, it depended on how worn out the pants were.

Dresses were the same. As she grew taller, the dresses got shorter, but those cute, little ruffled, decorative underpants were the perfect peek-a-boo look under the dress for Lisa. Then, when the dresses were too short for modesty sake, I was still able to have her wear them with a pair of matching slacks. I did whatever worked so that Lisa could wear some outfits a little longer.

Her age has always been deceiving; first, with her talking, and later, when she started walking. There were times when I had some difficulties taking her to a restaurant and being handed a children's menu when she wasn't in the age group listed on the menu. My dilemma was to either keep quiet and pay the reduced price, because it was their assumption on her age, or say "Excuse me, but she is older than what you guessed for her age." Most of the time I did the honest thing, and they would usually decide how to charge for her meals. I did think the regular meal was somewhat expensive for Lisa because she usually didn't eat much. Now, if it's mashed potatoes, that's a different story. She is known for eating way too much of mashed potatoes.

When she was older, with the first couple of jobs she interviewed for, the business personnel looked at her questionably. I would let them know before they asked that "Yes, she is old enough to be looking for a job." She was just short and young looking. I know, by law, they couldn't ask her age when interviewing her, but they asked other questions like, "Where do you work now, or what grade are you in?" She's pretty tolerant with people and their questions, but I've been known to be a little "short" (pun intended) with people. I have since realized that most people don't know any better, even some that should. It would be nice if size and age didn't matter quite so much, but all the major milestones are marked by age and the achievement. There are many milestones along the way that Lisa has reached and others that she has surpassed. As she has grown, she has learned to try everything that has been asked of her, and she has been able to accomplish many of her personal goals. Lisa's physical abilities started off with gaining muscle, stability and strength. Her constant, repetitive work in this area has paid off. Lisa is able to join in numerous physical activities and be a part of the fun. Her cognitive skills have also served her well, as she strived to learn the school curriculum set before her. She can read, write and understand the words set before her. She can do math, work with money and understand the intricate concepts. I truly believe she has withstood the test of time and has persevered.

A Letter From the Heart
Written in 1990

My dearest little Lisa,

First impressions can be misleading. I realized this when you were born and we were told of your disability. The doctor noted your funny creased eyelids, miniature nose and misplaced ears. He said you were lethargic and flaccid. Your tongue appeared too large for your mouth, and you had a straight line creased in the palm of your hands. The doctor said you had Down syndrome, but I did not understand what that syndrome was until he spoke the words "mongoloid and retarded." That was the moment I thought my world fell apart. I had visions of you unable to walk, talk or think. I had fears of an uncertain and dismal future. I was concerned of what others would say. I was afraid to love you, and cried a lot for you, for the family and for the dreadful future I had envisioned. I tried to deny such a thing could possibly happen to my child, but within days I had to admit what the doctors and tests positively revealed. You had Down syndrome.

You were unlucky enough to receive an extra 21st chromosome that affected you entirely, both physical and mental. You had trouble with breast-feeding, unable to suckle with enough strength to receive any milk. You would tire easily, fall asleep and miss many feedings. You were so tiny, and in the end I reluctantly gave in to using a bottle. You were very floppy and limp, and seemed content to just lie quietly and sleep. I was not coping well, struggling with all the emotions of having a new baby, a baby with a disability, a sickly baby and what doctors were saying about you and your heart.

They did not suggest an institution, thank goodness, but said to take you home, love you like any child needs to be loved, and think about special education when you were older.

While you were still in the hospital, I saw you desperately try to hold up your heavy head with your weak neck and shoulder muscles. This act was the encouragement I needed. You looked around at this cold, cruel world with your head bobbin', and then you quickly plopped face down on the bassinette mattress. You looked as if you were willing to try and so was I. From that moment on, I asked so much of you, always pushing you to try something new or to work a little harder when learning a skill. My theory was if I didn't set high expectations for you, how could I expect you to improve and be at your best?

I remember when you started school at the young age of three months. We had a teacher come to our home twice a week. She helped us to help you. We worked together to teach you how to lift your head up, hold it for a few seconds and maintain eye contact. We taught you to roll over, sit up and hold a spoon. Anything that other babies learned naturally, we all helped to teach you. I remember how we taught you to play with a new rattle, how to hold it, look at it and explore it with your hands and mouth. I exclaimed to the teacher that we taught you to put items in your mouth, only to have the next goal be how to place only appropriate items such as food in your mouth.

Lisa, being with you has been a roller coaster of events and emotions. You have survived your heart problems that required many trips to a specialist. We sat up many nights when you had many, many ear infections, bronchitis and pneumonia. You have survived numerous and frantic trips to the emergency room and subsequent hospitalizations. You had your heart procedure performed at eight months old to see how your heart was working, and over a few other years had four ear surgeries to have tubes inserted to help decrease ear infections. You certainly kept us on our toes.

Through it all you have continued to be a hard worker, trying anything new that we've asked of you. There were times when you would be very stubborn, but we still tried to help you and soon you ended up trying, too. You have affected many people, especially me. I now look at you as my daughter who has a disability, not as my handicapped daughter; that was my initial and erroneous thought when you were born. I can now see the best in others, trying to overlook any faults they may have. I can now see we all need to be different to make the world exciting and wonderful. I would not have asked for you to have Down syndrome, but you do, and I can love you deeply and unconditionally. You have taught me this.

I am so very proud of you and all your accomplishments so far in your life. I believe, with your capabilities, you will graduate from a high school, obtain a productive job in the community, and live on your own or with a friend, just as it should be. All my fears for your future were unfounded. You have already shown us just how capable you really are. I know you will continue to grow and learn. I love you, and I am very proud of you and your accomplishments. Best of all, I'm glad you are my daughter. Love, Mom

Epilogue

Now, fast forward to 2016. Lisa is an adult, living in an apartment with a close friend. We have truly come a long way since she was born. She kept us on our toes from the very beginning, but we soon formed a routine that helped us get through all those years of uncertainty and upheaval. I believe that it sounds worse than it was, because I am sure that as a family we just carried on, doing what had to be done. Lisa made it through grade school fairly unscathed. Sometimes feelings were hurt or emotions ran wild, depending on the situation. Yet, she survived those early years just in time to be ready for a move to a different state, a different school system and different potential friends.

She had a good transition into middle school followed by high school, with the help and support of a great staff of people willing to try new things because of Lisa. She had her first underage drink of alcohol, which would have never been discovered had she not put half of the container back in the refrigerator for us parents to find when we got home from a night out.

Lisa had several boyfriends, though some of those young men didn't even know they *were* her boyfriends. She had dates to dances and dates to go out to eat. She had her first job in the fast food industry at the age of sixteen, and held a second job in a grocery store during this same time, doing all this while attending high school. She was driven, motivated and determined. There were good times, great times and also disconcerting and scary times.

Lisa has experienced health issues, school issues and independence issues. But, she has also been very successful, too. I can't reveal all the details, but let's just say she met many of the goals she set for herself when she was in fourth grade, plus a few more. She is happy, well grounded and well adjusted. She is also powerful. And that is one of the stories you can look forward in a future book.

Thanks for reading!

Reference List

P. 2 [1] In humans, a single transverse palmar crease is a single crease that extends across the palm of the hand, formed by the fusion of the two palmar creases (known in the pseudoscience of palmistry as the "heart line" and the "head line") is found in half of people with Down syndrome. It is also found in 10% of the general population. Because it resembles the usual condition of non-human simians, it is also known as a simian crease or simian line, although these terms have widely fallen out of favor due to their pejorative connotation. Wikipedia 2015

P. 13 [2] CPR stands for cardiopulmonary resuscitation. It is an emergency lifesaving procedure that is done when someone's breathing or heartbeat has stopped. This may happen after an electric shock, heart attack, or drowning. CPR combines rescue breathing and chest compressions. From: MedlinePlus www.nlm.nih.gov 2016

P. 14 [3] Cardiac catheterization (cardiac cath or heart cath) is a procedure to examine how well your heart is working. A thin, hollow tube called a catheter is inserted into a large blood vessel that leads to your heart. From: American Heart Association www.heart.org 2016

P.14 [4] An echocardiogram uses sound waves to produce images of your heart. This commonly used test allows your doctor to see your heart beating and pumping blood. www.mayoclinic.org 2016

P. 19 [5] Homebound instruction can also be referred to as home teaching, home visits, and home or hospital instruction. Homebound instruction involves the delivery of educational services by school district personnel within a student's home. This differs from home schooling, which is usually delivered exclusively by a parent (Zirkel, 2003). www.brainline.org.

P. 27 [6] Prophylaxis is a Greek word and concept. It means any *action taken to guard or prevent beforehand.* From:simple.wikipedia.org 2016

P. 35 [7] A pincer grasp is grasp pattern emerging in the 10th-12th month whereby a small object is held between the distal pads of the opposed thumb and index or middle finger. http://medical-dictionary.thefreedictionary.com 2016

P. 77 [8] Speech & Language Therapy for Infants, Toddlers & Young Children www.ndss.org

P. 111 [9] *Life Goes On* was the first television series to have a major character with Down syndrome (Corky, played by Chris Burke). Aired on ABC from September 12, 1989, to May 23, 1993. (From Wikipedia)

P. 164 [10] According to what I remember, DLP, Developmental Learning Program is an educational program for students with disabilities in a regular education setting. Children are with age-appropriate peers and they work on an academic and useful daily living skills especially for them on an individual basis. In Lisa's case, her main classroom setting was DLP, and at certain times throughout the day she went to a typical, mainstream classroom, depending on the subject.

P. 167 [11] An Individualized Education Program (IEP) is a written statement of the educational program designed to meet a child's individual needs. Every child who receives special education services must have an IEP. From www.parentcenterhub.org .

P. 167 [12] The Individuals with Disabilities Education Act (IDEA) is a law ensuring services to children with disabilities throughout the nation. IDEA governs how states and public agencies provide early intervention, special education and related services to more than 6.5 million eligible infants, toddlers, children and youth with disabilities. From ED.gov

P.167 [13] Free Appropriate Public Education (FAPE) is an educational right of children with disabilities in the United States that is guaranteed by the Rehabilitation Act of 1973[1] and the Individuals with Disabilities Education Act (IDEA). From: Wikipedia

P. 167 [14] In basic terms, LRE, Least Restrictive Enviroment, refers to the setting where a child with a disability can receive an appropriate education designed to meet his or her educational needs, alongside peers without disabilities to the maximum extent appropriate. From: parentcenterhub.org

P.167 [15] Federal law defines an IEE, Independent Educational Evaluation, broadly as "an evaluation conducted by a qualified examiner who is not employed by the public agency responsible for the education of the child in question." 34 C.F.R. 300.503. From: http://www.wrightslaw.com

P.167 [16] The legal definition of ESY, Extended School Year services states that the term refers to special education and related services that are provided to a child with a disability, beyond the normal school year of the public agency, in accordance with the child's IEP and at no cost to the parents of the child, and that meet the standards of SEA (state educational agency.) From: Wikipedia

Resources

The Arc-For People with Intellectual and Developmental Disabilities   http://www.thearc.org

The Arc of Nebraska 3601 Calvert St Ste 25

Lincoln, NE 68506-5797

Website: www.arc-nebraska.org

Facebook: https://www.facebook.com/pages/The-Arc-of-Nebraska/167646211703

Phone: (402) 475-4407

Email: info@arc-nebraska.org Chapter #: 47

The Arc of Douglas County

2518 Ridge Ct Ste 238

Lawrence, KS 66046-4061

Website: www.thearcdcks.org

Facebook: https://www.facebook.com/pages/The-Arc-of-Douglas-County/208030402553129

Business Phone: (785) 749-0121

Chapter Email: bbishop@thearcdcks.org

Chapter #: 594

National Down Syndrome Society, 666 Broadway, 8th Floor, New York, New York,

http://www.ndss.org 1-800-221-4602

National Down Syndrome Congress

30 Mansell Court, Suite 108

Roswell, GA 30076

Toll free, at 1-800-232-NDSC (6372), Monday though Friday from 9:00 AM to 5:30 PM eastern time.

National Association for Down Syndrome

http://www.nads.org

1460 Renaissance Drive

Suite #405

Park Ridge, IL 60068

1-630-325-9112

Down Syndrome Guild of Greater Kansas City

http://www.kcdsg.org

5960 Dearborn St #100, Mission, KS 66202 Phone:(913) 384-4848

About the author

Angee Barcus is a wife, mother and author. She writes to help sort out issues that might otherwise fester and linger. Having a child with a disability was the last thing on her mind when Lisa was born. Before this fourth baby arrived, she was thinking more about all the dirty diapers and extra loads of clothes, as well as having to once again function on less hours of sleep at night.

After Lisa was born, her thoughts were quickly flooded with "what now" notions. Angee's nursing career allowed her to work in a school system, helping many young children who had developmental disabilities. This gave her another viewpoint about children with disabilities, which helped her when writing about Lisa.

Angee had a newspaper column that enlightened others about disability issues in and around where she lived, and she alternated those articles with short stories about Lisa. From that experience, she wrote this first book and has started on the second one about Lisa, sharing more of the same about Lisa's younger years and revealing some of the more difficult stories as Lisa has grown to adulthood.

www.ingramcontent.com/pod-product-compliance
Lightning Source LLC
Chambersburg PA
CBHW060150050426
42446CB00013B/2756